Colonial Settlements in America

Jamestown
New Amsterdam
Philadelphia
Plymouth
St. Augustine
Santa Fe
Williamsburg
Yerba Buena

Jamestown

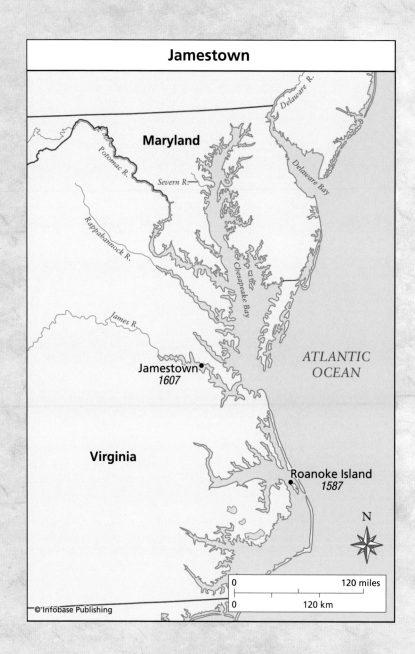

Maryland

Potomac R.

Severn R.

Rappahannock R.

Delaware R.

Delaware Bay

Chesapeake Bay

James R.

Jamestown
1607

ATLANTIC
OCEAN

Virginia

Roanoke Island
1587

N

0		120 miles
0	120 km	

Colonial Settlements in America

Jamestown

Tim McNeese

CHELSEA HOUSE PUBLISHERS

An imprint of Infobase Publishing

Frontis: Located on the James River, 30 miles from the Atlantic Ocean, the English settlement of Jamestown was established in 1607.

Jamestown

Copyright © 2007 by Infobase Publishing

For information contact:
Chelsea House
An imprint of Infobase Publishing
132 West 31st Street
New York NY 10001

ISBN-10: 0-7910-9335-2
ISBN-13: 978-0-7910-9335-1

Library of Congress Cataloging-in-Publication Data
McNeese, Tim.
    Jamestown / Tim McNeese.
        p. cm. — (Colonial settlements in America)
    Includes bibliographical references and index.
    Audience: Grades 7-8.
    ISBN 0-7910-9335-2 (hardcover)
    1. Jamestown (Va.)—History—Juvenile literature. 2. Virginia—History—Colonial
        period, ca. 1600-1775—Juvenile literature. I. Title. II. Series.
    F234.J3M38 2007
    973.2'1—dc22   2006028096

Chelsea House books are available at special discounts when purchased in bulk quantities for businesses, associations, institutions, or sales promotions. Please call our Special Sales Department in New York at (212) 967-8800 or (800) 322-8755.

You can find Chelsea House on the World Wide Web at http://www.chelseahouse.com

Series design by Erika K. Arroyo
Cover design by Ben Peterson

Printed in the United States of America

Bang FOF 10 9 8 7 6 5 4 3 2

This book is printed on acid-free paper.

All links and Web addresses were checked and verified to be correct at the time of publication. Because of the dynamic nature of the Web, some addresses and links may have changed since publication and may no longer be valid.

Contents

1

The Arrival of Strangers

Near the banks of a tidal stream the local residents called the Powhatan River, a Native American scout watched carefully into the distance. Nearby, the river's smooth waters flowed toward the east, the place where the great spirit rose each morning to light and warm the day. It was a spring day on the Chesapeake, and the year was 1607. The Native American scout was sitting in a tree where he could see farther than his companions who watched from the river's edge, taking care to keep themselves hidden in the bushes. From the ground to the branches where the scout was perched, the curious men talked between themselves in their native language, an Algonkian dialect. What exactly they were looking for they were not certain. But they would know it when they saw it. "It" would look like nothing they had ever seen before.

The Native Americans had heard of the strange people in their strange boats several days earlier. Their tribal leader, Wowinchopunk, had sent several scouting parties along the river to keep watch. As each group fanned out and took their places by the Powhatan, they remained close enough to the next group so that they could easily communicate up and down the hidden line. These scouting parties stationed themselves along the river, situated on its northern banks from the main village along the Chickahominy and the Powhatan all the way to Kecoughtan at the river's mouth. As the native watchers scanned downstream, each had his own thoughts. Who were these strangers? What would they look like? Would they speak a familiar language? Would they have anything to trade? What were they looking for? What did they want? How long would they stay? Would they be friends or enemies?

These Native Americans were extremely familiar with the places where they had taken up their posts. Along this portion of the river and stretching away from its banks into dark forests and woody swamps were the lands on which they lived. They belonged to a tribe called the Paspahegh. Theirs was a wonderful land, filled with open, fertile meadows and cool running streams. The forests seemed endless; woods filled with pines, hickories, oaks, cedars, maples, poplars, and black walnuts grew right up to the edge of the rivers. Their villages lined the Powhatan, as well as another river that flowed from the north. The main village of the Paspaheghs was situated where this second river (the modern-day Chickahominy) flowed into the Powhatan. That village had the same name as the tribe—Paspahegh—as it was the most important place where they lived. Paspahegh was also the name of a nearby island, which the tribe had, in earlier times, called their home. That spring, it was deserted. But it would soon be occupied by the people the Paspahegh men were waiting to see.

As the Paspahegh scouts watched from the north banks of the river, they were aware that they were not the only ones watching for the strangers. The lands of the Paspahegh did not extend on for a great distance. While they occupied the north banks, another tribe, the Quiyoughcohannock, made their home on the south banks. Up the Powhatan River were other tribes—the Weyanock, Appomattoc, and the Arrohattoc. To the north were the Chickahominy, Werowocomoco, Pamunkey, Youghtanund, and Mattaponi. Still others lived downriver, including the Warraskoyack, Kiskiack, and Nansemond. At the river's wide mouth was the Kecoughtan. They had already made contact with the strangers nearly two weeks earlier. That encounter had gone well. The Kecoughtans had met with the strangers and "entertained them very kindly."[1] An elderly Kecoughtan man had spoken to the strangers and delivered a long talk to them. He probably should not have bothered. The strange men could not understand a word of the Algonkian tongue nor were the Kecoughtans familiar with the words of the strangers. Perhaps it did not matter. The strangers had not remained with the Kecoughtans. They had pushed on upriver, still seemingly in search of something.

EARLIER ENCOUNTERS

Each of the tribes surrounding the Paspahegh was receiving word on the strangers. These tribes, approximately 30 of them, were not enemies of one another but allies. In part, the alliance between them had taken place because of another group of strangers. Nearly half a century earlier, in 1561, a small party of strangers had reached the Paspahegh villages. They were bearded men who spoke a foreign tongue. They had traded with the Paspahegh, and an important member of the tribe, Paquiquineo, agreed to accompany the strangers during their stay. This first encounter had ended peacefully.

Paquiquineo would experience many adventures alongside these strangers. He was led onboard one of their great ships, a vessel larger than the young man had ever seen before, and taken across a great ocean to their homeland—Spain. There, Paquiquineo met their leader, King Philip II of Spain. He became a favorite of the monarch. He was treated well by the Spanish and

During their exploration of what is today Virginia in the mid-1500s, the Spanish came in contact with many local Indian tribes, including the Paspahegh. One member of that tribe, Paquiquineo, was taken to Spain to meet King Philip II, who is depicted in this painting.

learned their language. He visited their cities and farms; their orchards and vineyards. He saw a whole new world. He was given a new name—Don Luis de Velasco, after the governor of Mexico. Although Paquiquineo enjoyed his life in the court of Philip II, he longed to return to his home. The following year, he was allowed to leave. He would accompany Spanish Jesuit priests who wanted to establish a mission along the Powhatan River to convert the Native Americans to Christianity. But during a visit to Mexico, Paquiquineo became ill with a fever and nearly died. Once he regained his health, he decided to remain in the Dominican convent, where his illness had been treated by the monks.

Even as the years passed, however, Paquiquineo wanted to return to his people. Finally, Spanish officials mounted an expedition to return to the Powhatan River, and he was included in their number. The party reached the Chesapeake region (the Spanish called Chesapeake Bay, "Bahia Santa Maria," the Bay of St. Mary). Mission buildings were erected near the Kiskiack Indian village on the Pamunkey River (the modern-day York River). Although the Spanish wanted Paquiquineo to remain with them and work at the mission, he had finally returned to his homeland and was thus eager to see his people. He left the Spanish fathers and went to live with one of his relatives in a village 30 miles upstream.

The Spanish Jesuits were disappointed and angered. They needed Paquiquineo to help protect their mission, because he could speak with the neighboring tribes. In fact, the mission was struggling to survive. There were serious food shortages and the local tribes refused to convert to Christianity. The Jesuit leader criticized Paquiquineo and insisted he return to the mission. He refused. When Father Juan Bautista de Segura sent men to capture Paquiquineo, they met resistance. Violence broke out, and two Spaniards were killed. Then, Paquiquineo and his people attacked the mission, killing all but a young servant boy. The Paspaheghs used the priests' axes to murder them.

When the Spanish learned of the attack, they dispatched four ships and 150 soldiers to the Chesapeake region. In the attacks that followed, Spanish soldiers killed 20 Paspaheghs and took 13 prisoner. One of Paquiquineo's uncles was killed. The Spanish military leader then told the Paspaheghs that they must give

Wahunsonacock (Chief Powhatan), depicted here in a detail of a map in one of John Smith's books about his explorations of Virginia, was the leader of the powerful Powhatan Confederacy at the time the English settled Jamestown. The confederacy consisted of approximately 30 tribes in what is now southeastern Virginia, the eastern shore of the Chesapeake Bay, and southern Maryland.

him Paquiquineo. When they refused, he hanged eight or nine of his captives "from the ship's rigging in clear view of any Indians looking on from the riverside."[2] But Paquiquineo never turned himself over to the Spanish. They had proven themselves to be ruthless men. Never again would the Native Americans along the Powhatan River be able to trust these bearded foreigners. (As for Paquiquineo, he disappeared from the historical record.)

It was this prolonged encounter that had led the various Indian tribes along the Powhatan and other rivers of the region to band together. Believing that the Spanish would return with greater numbers—more soldiers, more ships, more guns—they decided that they must become allies and fight the newcomers. A great alliance had been formed—the Powhatan Confederacy. By the 1570s, the leader of this confederacy was Wahunsonacock, who would be described as "strong . . . and of a daring spirit."[3] He was still leading the Powhatan Confederacy in the spring of 1607. The alliance had brought together the tribes living not only on the Powhatan River, but those north, as well. These tribes lived along other rivers—the Pamunkey, the Chickahominy, the Rappahannock, and the Patawomeck. All up and down the western shores of Chesapeake Bay, the tribal villages of the great Powhatan Confederacy were linked by water, spirit, and necessity.

NEW STRANGERS IN SIGHT

But the Spanish did not return. Other than occasional rumors of strangers, the Native Americans of the region had not had to face more bearded men—until the spring of 1607. Strangers had, indeed, arrived again, and they, too, had beards. Suddenly, the Native American scout in the tree shouted to his comrades: "There it comes."[4]

With great excitement, his fellow Paspaheghs crouched to avoid being seen and looked downstream. There, in the shadowy distance, were men in a small boat. The craft was known as a shallop, a boat not made for open waters, but for traveling the rivers. As the Paspaheghs watched, they saw that the men in the boat wore clothing unlike any among them. The men were light-skinned and the lower portion of their faces was covered with hair.

The Paspaheghs on both sides of the river continued to watch and made no overt gestures. They remained hidden as the bearded men used oars to row the shallop past them until they were out of sight. The strangers pushed their small boat past an island—Paspahegh—that would one day be their home. But even as they continued up the river, they came into view of more Paspaheghs hiding along the riverbanks. The strangers never left the sight of the anxious eyes of dozens of Paspahegh men.

Eight days later, the shallop returned and passed Paspahegh Island again, moving back downstream. In another three days, the strangers returned, this time in greater numbers, onboard three larger boats—ships that had brought them from across the sea to this remote corner of North America. This time, they did not pass but brought their vessels alongside the island, then tied ropes to the trees to secure their ships. The following morning, the island was covered with more than 100 men. As the Paspaheghs continued watching them, the new, bearded strangers unloaded their ships, bringing their supplies and foodstuffs to shore. They began cutting down trees. They were building a fort for protection. Even though they could not see the people who were constantly watching them, the strangers knew they were there. But these strangers were not Spaniards; they were Englishmen.

For the Paspaheghs, some of their questions were already being answered. The strangers looked much like others who had arrived years earlier. They spoke an unknown language. As they built their fort, it was clear they intended to stay.

2

A New World Rivalry

Even as the Paspaheghs watched the bearded strangers mov-ing along the Powhatan River, they were unaware that men like these had begun exploring the New World more than a century earlier. In the early morning hours of October 12, 1492, a Spanish flotilla of only three small ships had spotted land that was part of a continent they had not even known existed. The ships were sponsored by the Spanish monarchs, King Ferdinand and Queen Isabella, and their captain was one of the most famous explorers in history—Christopher Columbus. Columbus had reached a small island in the Bahamas, and the history of the world was about to change forever. A new world had been "discovered" by Europeans. (Not that it was an entirely unknown world, because American Indians had been living in it for thousands of years.) Although Columbus never realized he had failed in his attempt to reach the Far East, with its highly prized spices, silks, and other valuables, he had not found Asia by sailing west across the Atlantic Ocean. He had found the Americas.

This painting by Dióscoro Téofilo de la Puebla depicts the landing of Christopher Columbus at San Salvador, or Watling Island, on October 12, 1492. Although Columbus failed to discover a route to the Far East, his arrival in the Americas signaled the beginning of European conquest of the New World.

SPANISH NEW WORLD

Columbus's failure to discover a route to the Far East would soon become Spain's success. For much of the next century, Spanish officials followed up on the explorer's discoveries. They established a New World empire that they ruled exclusively. Through additional expeditions by other explorers (Columbus would continue his own explorations for another decade), the Spanish claimed lands that stretched from the equator to as far north as Florida on the Atlantic Ocean and California on the Pacific Ocean.

During the 1500s, the king of Spain not only dominated much of the New World but also would control the shipping between the Western Hemisphere and the European continent. This created a strong rivalry between the Spanish and at least three other European powers of western Europe—the Dutch, the French, and the British. All three of these nations had only recently developed into important sea powers in Europe. But each was ready by the late 1500s to challenge the strong Spanish hold on New World wealth and trade. By 1580, the English, for example, were significantly expanding their trade connections around the world. They were sailing to more places on more ships than ever before. As the English further challenged Spanish power and dominance in the Western Hemisphere during these years, conflict with Spain increased. In some instances, challenging the Spanish in the New World amounted to little more than piracy. English, Dutch, and sometimes French sailing crews plied the high seas near Spanish sea-lanes as privateers, willing to challenge a Spanish treasure ship and steal its cargo. In the case of English privateers, many were paid and supported by London merchants who wanted to expand their markets.

Oftentimes, these European challenges to Spanish power in the New World went beyond piracy. The English, for example, were intent on discovering an easy, all-water route around or through the American landmass to complete the original goal set by Christopher Columbus. They were searching for a waterway through the continent to the Orient, which had its own riches and potentially valuable cargoes. The route came to be known as the "Northwest Passage." (The Spanish already controlled what could be called a "Southwest Passage" around the southern tip of South America, but they restricted access by other countries. This route was long and treacherous, but it provided the Spanish with a route to the Pacific and the Orient.)

By the 1580s, the English and the Spanish were fighting one another in a long-range sea war, which would last until 1604. One aspect of this conflict was the strong animosity that existed between Spanish Catholics and English Protestants. This combined religious, economic, and geographical rivalry reached its high watermark when Philip II, the Spanish king, sent a large

SPANISH POWER AND NEW WORLD GOLD

Once Christopher Columbus made his "discovery" of the New World at the end of the fifteenth century, the Spanish immediately set out to establish the first European empire in the Americas. Over the next 50 years, Spanish explorers and soldiers, called *conquistadors*, had made further discoveries from the modern-day American Southwest to Florida and from Mexico to South America. By the 1540s, the result of these numerous explorations was a chain of colonies. Each was centrally and tightly organized, and run by Spanish officials who sought to bring honor and wealth to their monarch. While the Spanish wanted to establish a New World kingdom that was a financial success, they also wanted to convert the American natives to Christianity. The Spanish poured money into their colonies, and the rewards would prove extraordinary. They would support Catholic missionaries and conquistadors, who sought out new lands and people for Spain to exploit. The Spanish Empire would include peoples who had accumulated vast wealth, such as the Aztecs in modern-day Mexico and the Incas in today's Peru.

The gold and silver they pilfered from these empires and other American natives was staggering. The Spanish also ordered the natives to work silver and gold mines, forcing them to produce even greater wealth in the name of the Spanish king. Throughout much of the second half of the 1500s, Spanish treasure ships delivered their cargoes of gold home to Spain, making the Spanish kingdom one of the wealthiest in European history. These great treasure ships were filled to the gunwales with precious metals and exotic products, such as hardwoods, all of which were highly prized in Spain. Modern historians estimate that Spanish treasure ships delivered 18,000 tons of silver and 200 tons of gold to Spain from their New World colonies between 1521 and 1600.* The Spanish port of Seville became one of the wealthiest in all of Europe.

In the meantime, the leaders of other European countries looked on with envy. When explorers and sea captains sailed to the Americas on behalf of their monarchs and merchants, they wanted to reap the same benefits as the Spanish. They, too, sought gold and other metal riches. It would be one of the first objects the founders of Jamestown set their sights on. Unfortunately, the English colonists never found the golden riches in their colonies that had made the Spanish New World empire so wealthy and enviable.

---

*Tim McNeese, *The Reformation* (St. Louis, Mo.: Milliken Publishing Company, 1999), 18.

flotilla of warships to invade England in 1588. Fortunately for the English, they were able to meet the challenge of the Spanish Armada. In sea battles that took place in July, the English outfought the Spanish, causing the armada to lose 40 ships and thousands of Spanish troops. This defeat produced a serious crack in the veneer of Spanish domination of the Atlantic and of the New World.

ENGLISH COLONIES ON THE HORIZON

By August 1604, the rivalry between the English and Spanish had largely come to an end. That year, the English king, James I, signed a treaty with the Spanish government. London merchants had sought an agreement from Spain to recognize the right of the English to deliver their ships to Spanish colonies for the purpose of trade. That attempt had failed; it would not be part of the English-Spanish treaty. However, it did not stop the English from sailing their merchant ships to the Caribbean in defiance of Spanish authority. There, they traded, even if illegally. One such sea captain was "Christopher Newport of Limehouse, Mariner."[5] Newport had first sailed into the West Indies of the Caribbean in 1589. Sometimes he had been seeking trade; other times he had been engaged as a privateer and raider. His reputation had become quite far-flung as "a Mariner well practiced for the Westerne parts of America."[6] With this reputation, it is not surprising that, in 1607, he was selected as the commander of the English expedition that sailed up the Powhatan River.

Over the last two decades of the sixteenth century, the English and Spanish competed against one another over trade in the New World. Despite the immense power represented by the Spanish colonies in the Americas, the English were a confident people. In 1558, they had crowned a new monarch, Queen Elizabeth, one of the daughters of King Henry VIII. She was an extremely intelligent and politically wise woman, one loved by the vast majority of her subjects. Her reign lasted for more than 40 years. During those years, she supported the arts and sciences, including some of the greatest writers, painters, and composers in England's history—William Byrd, Edmund Spenser, and William Shakespeare. She also supported English trade abroad, as well as efforts to colonize across the seas. Only the Spanish offered a formidable obstacle to overseas expansion. When, in 1588, English ships stopped the attack by the Spanish Armada, it appeared that this small island nation in the North Atlantic might be able to surpass even Spain as a world power. It was a time when England and its royal ruler, whom many referred to as "Good Queen Bess," were emerging as a world power.

Even before the defeat of the Spanish Armada, Englishmen had made their first serious attempts to establish colonies of their own in North America. It all began during the mid-1580s. By that time, the Spanish Empire had gained a foothold in the Caribbean, in modern-day Mexico, and lands that would one day become part of the United States, such as Florida. The English had already explored North America. In 1496, Queen Elizabeth's grandfather Henry VII had dispatched a Genoese sea captain named John Cabot on a single ship to explore the northern coast of the New World. Cabot sailed through the cold waters of the North Atlantic and reached modern-day Canada, which he called the "new found land" (today's Newfoundland). Upon Cabot's return, King Henry VII was so pleased that he sent him back, this time with four ships. However, this English venture into North American exploration ultimately went no-where. Cabot and his ships disappeared in 1498 and were never heard from again.

Other failures followed. In 1501, Henry sent a company of ships bearing both English and Portuguese merchants to New-foundland. They were to establish trade connections and search for the Northwest Passage. They failed at both. Eight years later, Cabot's son, Sebastian, followed up on his father's earlier ex-ploration. But, by then, Henry VIII had risen to the throne.

In 1496, King Henry VII of England backed Italian explorer
John Cabot's venture to find a direct link to the Far East. The
following year, when he landed in present-day Newfoundland,
Cabot (depicted here) became the first European explorer
since the Vikings to reach the North American mainland.

Although *this* Henry spent a good deal of money building up England's trade network and fishing fleets, he did not use them to establish a colony in Newfoundland. He had little interest in New World explorations. Through the decades that followed, English ships were sent each spring to North American waters not to explore or colonize but to fish. The Grand Banks off the coast of Newfoundland and neighboring Nova Scotia were home to countless codfish. The fish were caught, salted, and sold in large barrels. But, while the trade produced great profits, it produced no permanent English colony in North America.

3

A Toehold in North America

By the 1580s, with Queen Elizabeth on the throne, the direction taken by the English in North America began to change. English fishermen were casting their nets along the Grand Banks, while English privateers were casting theirs in search of Spanish treasure ships to attack. Some of these privateers had the ear of Good Queen Bess; they were gentlemen in Elizabeth's court. They included aristocrats such as Sir Walter Ralegh and Sir Humphrey Gilbert. (Though his name is usually written Sir Walter Raleigh, he consistently spelled his name "Ralegh.") In addition, the sons of wealthy merchants, such as John Hawkins and Francis Drake, participated in these raids as well. These men—called "sea dogs"—became favorites of the queen through their sea raids against the Spanish. They all wanted to "singe [King Philip's] beard."[7] Each established his own reputation for preying on the Spanish. John Hawkins raided from the coast of West Africa to the Spanish-controlled islands of the Caribbean until he was killed in a sea battle against the Spanish off the Mexican coast near the Yucatan.

In the latter decades of the 1500s, Queen Elizabeth I of England commissioned privateers to raid Spanish treasure ships in the New World. One of Elizabeth's favorite privateers was Sir Francis Drake, who is depicted here in the queen's court by British artist Frank Moss Bennett.

Next, Elizabeth dispatched Francis Drake in 1577. Drake had already engaged in raids against the Spanish a few years earlier. Among his most daring was an attack on a mule train along the coast of Panama that netted Drake a fortune in Peruvian silver. But his greatest exploits were yet to come. Commanding six ships, he became a terror to the Spanish. Their treasure ships were "like chickens caught in a hen house by a fox."[8] Commanding from the deck of his flagship, the *Golden*

Hind, Drake became legendary. He attacked Spanish ports in Central America and raided settlements along the coast of South America, including Valparaiso, Chile, and Lima, Peru. When he believed Spanish ships would be waiting for him on his return to Caribbean waters, Drake chose to sail around the southern tip of the continent. After considering a colony near the site of modern-day San Francisco (he met with local Native Americans to work out a deal), Drake sailed out into the vast South Sea—the Pacific Ocean—to the Philippines, yet another Spanish target. His voyage would take him around the world. He sailed around Africa and returned to Elizabeth's court with a huge cargo of East Indian spices and Spanish silver.

THE ENGLISH LOOK TO NORTH AMERICA

While treasure reached English coffers through the daring deeds of their "sea dogs," such ventures were expensive and hardly paid for themselves. Spain was still the dominant power in the Americas. By the early 1580s, another of Elizabeth's courtiers, Sir Humphrey Gilbert, convinced her to pursue a different strategy in the New World. Gilbert suggested that raiding was not the answer. Instead, he would establish a series of military colonies along the North American coast, "a kind of picket line,"[9] to keep the Spanish from moving farther north from Florida. These colonists would also establish friendly relations with local Native Americans and trade with them. The English would convert them to Protestant Christianity (the Spanish were converting the Native Americans to Catholicism). In the meantime, Gilbert would use such colonies as bases of support while he searched for North American treasure. No one had yet discovered vast quantities of gold and silver in the north as the Spanish had in the south. But Gilbert was certain he would be the first. Queen Elizabeth had her lawyers draw up a contract for colonization with Sir Humphrey. The English were going to colonize North

America at last. And Gilbert's contracts would grant him the sole right to colonize there in the name of the queen.

But things did not go well for Gilbert. The queen did not agree to pay for his efforts to establish colonies. His contract with the Crown did help him find willing investors, however. One of those investors was Sir Walter Ralegh. Gilbert was able to raise a small fleet of ships and made plans to sail to North America. His first attempt failed completely as his ships did not even reach America before turning back. Then, in 1583, he managed to reach Newfoundland with three small ships. There, he claimed land for his queen, which he named St. John's. Unfortunately, the luckless Gilbert and his tiny New World fleet were soon lost at sea in a violent storm.

Once word of the demise of Gilbert and his fleet reached England, another of Elizabeth's courtiers stepped forward. Walter Ralegh soon petitioned the queen for permission to take over Gilbert's contract to explore and colonize North America. He was, after all, Gilbert's half brother. The queen agreed. Ralegh spent the next 20 years planning a trip to establish a colony in North America. But he did not wait long to take his first steps. Unlike Gilbert, Ralegh would not go to the New World himself. He would send others. Ralegh assembled "a remarkable group of men who brought together scientific knowledge and practical experience."[10] They would include an Oxford scientist, Thomas Harriot; John White, a young artist; and Philip Amadas and Arthur Barlowe, both excellent seamen. Ralegh sent these men and others on two small boats to the southern American coast during the summer of 1584. Ralegh had selected a spot to establish a colony along the mid-Atlantic coast. It is not clear why he chose this location. He may have been trying to avoid the problems his half brother encountered farther north. He may also have been interested in establishing a colony to meet the challenge of the Spanish to the south head-on. Such a colony could serve as a launching point for additional raids against

In the 1580s, English explorer Sir Walter Ralegh attempted to establish a colony along what is today the coast of North Carolina. In 1584, he dispatched captains Philip Amadas and Arthur Barlowe to explore Roanoke Island, where he hoped to establish this colony. Amadas and Barlowe are depicted here with a group of Native Americans on Roanoke Island.

Spanish silver ships. This was an important part of the colonizing plan. One could not depend on profits scratched out of the wilderness by a tiny English outpost. But the capture of a single Spanish silver ship might yield a prize worth 10 or 15 thousand pounds; perhaps two or three times that amount.

Harriot, White, and the others selected a spot along the modern-day North Carolina coast, between the Pamlico and Albemarle sounds called the Outer Banks. Between those two bays, they reached an island they called Roanoke. Things looked so promising for the new colony that the new arrivals decided to name the lands they occupied Virginia, in honor of the Virgin

Queen. (Elizabeth had never married.) But, even as the boats reached the island, Native Americans were watching them from the mainland.

RALEGH AND ROANOKE

This first voyage to Roanoke Island was merely a scouting mission. However, the following year, Ralegh dispatched more than 100 colonists to the island under the command of Ralph Lane, a professional soldier. Lane was excited about what he saw when he landed at Roanoke. He reported back to England in September 1585 that the colony was located on "the goodliest and most pleasing territorie of the world."[11] The local Native Americans were supportive, the climate was mild, and there was little sickness among the colonists. (New World illnesses, especially fevers, were a common problem in such colonies.) Lane believed that, if the colony succeeded, "no realme in Christendome" could rival it.[12]

Despite their excitement about the colony's potential, the colonists expected to find gold on the lands they occupied. One of the members of their party, Joachim Ganz, was a Jewish mineral expert, who was supposed to search for gold and silver. To transplant English society in the New World, the colonists also included not only carpenters and farmers but winemakers and druggists.

All did not remain well at Roanoke. Building the colony was difficult work. There were frequent storms, and the colonists had arrived too late in the year to plant crops for food. Despite hopeful beginnings, the colonists and the local Native Americans clashed. The colonists relied on native gifts of food for too long, and the Native Americans became anxious about their own food stores running low. When the Native Americans cut off food to the colonists, Ralph Lane chose to attack a local village in the spring of 1586, killing the chief of the Roanokes. This set the colonists and Roanokes permanently against one another. That summer, the nearly starved colonists were picked up by Francis Drake, who happened to be in the area.

Ralegh's attempt to colonize Roanoke in 1585 and 1586 had collapsed, but the intrepid colonizer was not completely discouraged. He planned again and soon mounted another colonizing enterprise. While he had only opened his original colony to men, this time he allowed women and children as well. By the spring of 1587, everything was again in place. He had lined up 150 men, plus their family members, including two wives who were pregnant. Some of the recruits were part of the first trip, such as the artist John White, who signed on again. (White and Thomas Harriot had produced a book titled *Brief and True Report of the New Found Land of Virginia*, which White had illustrated. It served as an advertisement for recruitment.) The new colony was to be named "The City of Ralegh in the Colony of Virginia." Ralegh even had a special coat of arms commissioned for his New World "city." In April, the party set sail for America. They were not to return to the same location as the earlier colony, however. The ship's captain, Simon Fernandez, was to land the party north of Roanoke Island, somewhere in the Chesapeake Bay region. However, Fernandez dumped the colonists off near the original Roanoke site, so he could sail south and engage in a raid against Spanish silver ships.

This change in plans was only the first of many problems experienced by the new Roanoke colony. As with the earlier colony, the English colonists arrived too late to plant a food crop. Too many of them spent too much time searching for gold. Supplies ran extremely low. The colonists begged White to return to England and bring back fresh supplies. White agreed but postponed his departure until his married daughter gave birth to his grandchild. The baby girl was named Virginia Dare. She was the first English baby born in the New World.

But when White returned to England for much-needed supplies, he was soon caught up in an international crisis. War broke out between Spain and England. In time, the Spanish monarch, King Philip II, sent his armada to attack England. Needing all available ships, the Crown would not allow White

THE POPHAM COLONY

During the 1580s, several attempts were made to establish a permanent English colony in North America. Each failed miserably. Following the collapse of the second Roanoke colony during the late 1580s, Sir Walter Ralegh abandoned any further colonial efforts along the shores of his newly named "Virginia." The remainder of the sixteenth century passed, and no new colonizing attempts were mounted.

But the New World continued to present a challenge for the English. The Spanish continued their successes in the Caribbean, as well as Central and South America, while the French were having limited success in modern-day Canada, lands they called New France. The English watched these successes jealously. In time, new colonizing endeavors were begun. By 1602, the English were again on their way to America. But not to Virginia or the lands to the south. These new colonists headed north.

This new attempt to build an English colony in America was centered in the region of modern-day Massachusetts and Maine. Far off the coast of this region, English fishermen had been harvesting great catches of codfish for several decades. Inland, these new English colonial traders and settlers were interested in getting involved in the fur trade. And, on a smaller scale, they also planned to harvest cedar trees.

But these new efforts would prove just as difficult and shaky as those attempted at Roanoke. The English continued to have problems with local Native Americans. Usually the English were to blame; they often mistreated the Nauset, the local tribe they traded with. One of the traders, a merchant named Martin Pring, even threatened them with two mastiffs, a pair of giant dogs named Fool and Gallant. Pring soon "wore out his welcome."*

An additional example of mismanagement can be seen in an English effort launched in 1605. That year, an English merchant named George Weymouth made his way to modern-day Maine. He wanted to establish a trading post to buy and barter with the local Abenaki Indians. But the Abenakis were not interested in trading with Weymouth. They had already formed long-standing trade connections with the French on the other side of the St. Lawrence River to the north. Weymouth then took unnecessary to leave for Roanoke until 1590. Once he made his way back to his Virginia colony, it was too late. The colony was abandoned, and all the colonists he had left behind, including his daughter,

---

and desperate steps. Refusing to take "no" for an answer from the Abenakis, he lured some of them onto his ship and seized them by the hair, taking five of them as prisoners. He then abandoned the region entirely and returned to England with his captives.

The following year, another party of English merchants returned to Maine. They brought with them three of the five Abenaki prisoners taken by Weymouth. These new traders had important backing. They were financed by a group of wealthy investors called the Plymouth Company. This group had gained the privilege to colonize between Maine and the Potomac River in modern-day Virginia. A second group of investors had been granted lands of their own to the south. Their grant included the region lying between modern-day New York City and North Carolina. (This claim would include the lands that Ralegh had tried to colonize during the 1580s.)

The backing for the new colony was provided by an English judge named Sir John Popham. The leader of this new group of traders and colonizers was Martin Pring. He selected the site for the colony's new trading post at the mouth of the Kennebec River. The site was known to the local Native Americans as Sagadahoc. By the following year, new leaders arrived, including George Popham, a relative of Sir John, and Ralegh Gilbert, the 24-year-old son of Sir Humphrey Gilbert. Problems continued to plague the colony. A fire destroyed much of the colony's supplies. George Popham died before the end of the first winter. Relations with the local tribes continued to move from bad to worse. Again, the English were largely to blame.

The colony ultimately collapsed under its own poor leadership and the effects of starvation. Half of the colony's members died during the winter season. Those who survived the harsh winter of 1607–08 built a small ship weighing 30 tons and sailed back to Plymouth, England. By that time, another colony had been established in Virginia, one that would ultimately survive—Fort James.

---

*Peter Charles Hoffer, *The Brave New World: A History of Early America* (Boston: Houghton Mifflin Company, 2000), 119.

In 1587, 100 English colonists under the command of Governor John White established a colony at Roanoke Island. When the colony ran short of supplies, White left for England but was detained by the Spanish Armada. Upon his return in 1590, White found the colony abandoned, and the only trace he discovered was the mysterious word Croatoan, which was written on a nearby tree.

son-in-law, and grandchild, had vanished. On a tree, he discovered the word CROATOAN carved into the wood. (The Croatan was a local Indian tribe.) Even today, no one is certain what happened to the colonists. History would refer to this second effort by Ralegh to colonize in the Americas as "The Lost Colony of Roanoke."

Yet even before the news of the "Lost Colony" reached Sir Walter Ralegh back in England, he had already decided to give up New World colonizing altogether. Much money had been spent, and his efforts had produced nothing. There were no riches to be had in North America, he decided. By 1589, Ralegh formally transferred his rights to establish a New World colony to a group of 19 investors. The majority of them were wealthy London merchants. But these new investors made no sudden moves toward America. They studied their options and bided their time. The sixteenth century came to an end, yet still no new attempt was made to establish a colony. Ralegh himself knew what the problem was. He wrote: "No man makes haste to the market where there is nothing to be bought but blows."[13]

4

Bound for the New World

The earliest English attempts to establish a colony in North America had taken place during the reign of Queen Elizabeth I. She had been a supporter of those efforts and provided the necessary royal permissions for would-be colonists. But Elizabeth's role in New World colonization would come to an end early in the 1600s. The queen died in the spring of 1603. Torch-lit barges carried her embalmed body down the Thames River in London on March 26 to give her subjects one last opportunity to pay their respects to Good Queen Bess. Since she had never married, the queen had no child to take the throne at her death. Instead, royal rule passed to King James VI of Scotland, who would be crowned as James I of England. King James did not wish to continue the ongoing sea conflicts with Spain. He soon agreed to a treaty, condemning the acts of privateers, and promising to halt the English raids on Spanish silver ships. But he was not going to give up English claims to the North American mainland north of Spanish Florida.

During his reign (1603–1625), King James I established peace with Spain but still supported England's colonization of America. In 1606, King James granted a charter to the Virginia Company to establish a settlement at Jamestown, which was named in his honor.

COLONIAL ORGANIZERS

James gave his support to important English leaders and wealthy merchants from London, as well as port towns such as Plymouth and Bristol. They wanted to establish new colonies along the Atlantic seacoast. Sir John Popham was one of these eager and important leaders. Another was Sir Thomas Smythe, head of the East India Company, one of the most significant of all English trading businesses. The details of how the new colony, the one that would become Jamestown, originally took shape are not clear. But three names stand out in the early plans to bring about a new colony situated in the New World's "Virginia."

One was Bartholomew Gosnold. Jamestown colonist Captain John Smith described Gosnold as "one of the first movers" of the Virginia colony.[14] Gosnold's family was well known and had important connections. (He was married to a cousin of Sir Thomas Smythe.) He had a reputation as a privateer and explorer. He had made a trip to New England in 1602 to trade for furs and cedarwood. Here was a colonial organizer who had already visited the shores of North America.

The second important figure was Gosnold's cousin Edward Maria Wingfield. He, too, had the right connections with important people, including Sir Ferdinando Gorges. He and Gorges had met in 1588, when they were both prisoners of a war the English were fighting in French Flanders. Wingfield was important enough that his name would be among those whom the king would grant a charter, or royal permission, to establish a new colony in America.

The third leader in the early plans to establish a New World colony was perhaps the most important of them all. He was not from an influential family like Wingfield or Gosnold. He was the son of a Lincolnshire farmer. Deciding that farming life was not for him, he had turned to a military career early in life. He was a veteran of foreign wars, having fought in northern France and the Netherlands. He had served in the army of Archduke Ferdinand of Austria and fought the Turks in eastern Europe. When he returned to England after five years of fighting overseas, he was a battle-seasoned veteran. His name was Captain John Smith.

These three men were at the center of organizing a new colony in America. They managed to convince "certaine of the

Along with Bartholomew Gosnold and Edward Maria Wingfield, Captain John Smith was one of the primary leaders of the Jamestown settlement. Prior to leaving for Jamestown in December 1606, Smith spent several years as a mercenary for France and the Habsburg Empire.

Nobilitie, Gentry, and Marchants,"[15] wrote Smith, to bankroll their colonial enterprise by the summer of 1605. Among these investors were Sir John Popham (who, by 1607, would give his support to another colony farther north that would be named for him) and King James's first minister, Robert Cecil. Popham and Cecil, with support from the Crown, brought together a powerful group of merchants as backers. These merchants from Plymouth and Bristol were interested in the profits that could be made from fish, furs, and timber in New England. London merchants saw the potential for making a profit in raising such crops as tobacco, hops, hemp, and flax, which was used to make linen cloth.

Ultimately, these organizing efforts led to the establishment of two groups of investors and two colonies. Lord Popham drew up the appropriate papers by April 10, 1606. The result was the formation of two companies. The "Virginia Company of Plymouth" was made up of merchants from "West Country," including Plymouth, Bristol, and Exeter. Their colony would include the lands between latitudes 38 and 45 degrees north. These lands stretched from modern-day northern Maine south to the Chesapeake Bay at the Potomac River. The other company, the "Virginia Company of London," was granted the region between latitudes 34 and 41 degrees north. This included the territory from modern-day Cape Fear, North Carolina, north to where New York City would one day be located. (Some of the territory of the two colonies overlapped, between latitudes 38 degrees and 41 degrees. This region would be shared.) From the northernmost point of the Plymouth group's colony to the southernmost point of the London group's colony was a vast extent of 900 miles of wilderness, waiting to challenge the English and their colonial plans.

The appropriate permissions were now in place. From the beginning, the organizers of the colony knew they needed to establish a permanent settlement in the New World, not just a trading post. Plans were well laid out. The company men would recruit the appropriate number of colonists first. They would acquire the ships, stock them with provisions, and hire a captain and crew. Once the colonists reached the New World, they would build a fort for protection. A larger settlement would surely follow. The colonists would be expected to fish and raise crops. They would trade with the local Native Americans. Some of the colonists would explore the rivers and inlets of the region in search of the "Northwest Passage." They would make maps of every place they explored. The new colonists were to also keep an eye out for any survivors of the "Lost Colony of Roanoke." Christopher Newport, known as a "well practiced" sea captain, was hired to command the small fleet.

READY TO SAIL

Just a few days after Christmas 1606, the colonists seemed ready to embark for the New World. They were to sail on three small ships. The largest was the *Susan Constant*. It weighed 120 tons and was a merchant vessel. It was also heavily armed, and was "packed to the gunnels with supplies."[16] The *Susan Constant* was to be the "admiral" vessel, the name given the lead ship. It carried 71 colonists and crewmen and was captained by Christopher Newport. The colonists could not have been led by a better seaman. Newport had been to the Americas many times. He had engaged in raids against the Spanish and "knew as much about American waters as any Englishman alive."[17] He was to command the entire three-ship fleet until the vessels reached Virginia.

The second ship was the *Godspeed*. Its captain was Bartholomew Gosnold, one of the colony's three leaders. This vessel was less than half the size of the *Susan Constant*, perhaps 40 tons. It would carry 52 men. The third ship was hardly a ship

During their trip to Virginia, the Jamestown colonists traveled on three ships: the *Susan Constant*, *Godspeed*, and *Discovery*. The journey across the Atlantic Ocean took approximately four months and after some exploration of the Chesapeake Bay region, the Jamestown colony was established on May 14, 1607. Pictured here are replicas of the *Susan Constant*, *Godspeed*, and *Discovery* at the Jamestown National Historic Site.

at all. It was a small pinnace, the *Discovery*, of only 20 tons. (A pinnace is a small sailing boat designed to deliver men and supplies from one ship to another or from a ship to land.) John Ratcliffe was to be its captain. Although small, the *Discovery* carried 21 men who took their places "on her decks wherever they could find space in between the clutter of provisions and equipment."[18] They numbered 144 men total—colonists and

(continues on page 42)

THE ENGLISH WAY OF COLONIZING

The English model for colonizing the New World would always be different from the way the Spanish established their colonies. Spanish monarchs provided the monies and financed nearly every colonial effort. This meant that the profits generated from Spanish colonies usually went into the coffers of the king back in Spain. The English monarchs only supported colonization by granting permission and by agreeing to contracts and charters that gave would-be colonists a certain piece of land to colonize. At that point, English royal support came up short. The money needed to finance a colony was raised privately, usually by investment companies. The Virginia Companies are two examples. In structure, these companies were called "joint-stock companies." Merchants sold shares of stock to investors who were willing to put money into the enterprise. They did so hoping that the colony would eventually make a profit, giving them a return on their investment. The money raised through the purchase of stock shares was used to buy ships, supplies, and to recruit colonists and crews.

The group of colonists who signed on for the expedition to the New World in 1606 was a varied mix of Englishmen. (No women or children were included in the original party.) Some had enough money to pay their own passage. Poorer colonists joined the group as indentured servants. Unable to pay, they agreed to work off a seven-year "indenture" to cover the cost of the ship voyage. Some of the most skilled colonists were those who were not members of the aristocracy:

> Among the nongentry were a dozen skilled craftsmen and artisans—a blacksmith, a mason, two bricklayers, four carpenters, a tailor, two barbers, and a surgeon; the rest of the company was made up of unskilled workers of various kinds: common seamen, laborers, and boys. The majority of men whose origins have been traced were from the southern and eastern regions of England, especially from London and its surrounding counties.*

* James Horn, *A Land as God Made It: Jamestown and the Birth of America* (New York: Basic Books, 2005), 48.

(continued from page 40)

sailors—who sailed from the Blackwell docks of East London, down the Thames River on December 30, 1606. They were bound to the open sea toward a world many of them could only imagine.

5

Settlement and Exploration

The description of the voyage across the Atlantic begins to tell the story of the difficulties experienced by those who would settle the Jamestown colony. The ships had to remain docked at Kent for six weeks due to storms. The men were at odds with one another and on edge due to their cramped quarters and sea-tossed ships. Even before England faded into the distance and the ships sailed away, the colonists were fighting among themselves. John Smith found himself in the middle of the infighting. He gave so much advice to Newport and Wingfield that they began to dislike him, thinking him to be "nothing more than a young upstart and braggart, a man who spent too much time questioning and not enough following orders."[19] Smith, for his part, began to think of Wingfield as incompetent and arrogant. By mid-February, Smith's insults and second-guessing led to an accusation of mutiny against him, and he was "restrained as a prisoner."[20] Things were not going well, and the colonists had not even reached the North American coast.

Before arriving in Virginia, Newport had decided to sail his ships to the Caribbean. In the islands, the colonists could take on fresh supplies. There they also rested for several days and took baths in natural hot and cold springs. They spent time hunting and fishing, as well. Smith remained under arrest during this time, and Captain Newport decided to make Smith's insubordination an example and ordered a "paire of gallows" constructed. Smith was to hang. But Gosnold intervened on Smith's behalf. Smith was spared, which was fortuitous for the would-be colonists.

BOUND FOR VIRGINIA

By April 10, Captain Newport sailed his ships northward. Eleven days out, the colonists faced a violent storm that lasted through an entire night "with winds, raine, and thunders in a terrible manner."[21] One of the ship captains, John Ratcliffe, announced he was ready to abandon their planned trip to Virginia and return to England. But the storm finally passed and less than a week later, the three English ships came within sight of the coast of Virginia. On April 26, the ships "entred into the Bay of Chesupioc [Chesapeake] directly, without any let or hindrance."[22] The colonists were relieved to have finally arrived. They had only lost one man so far. Soon, Newport, Wingfield, and Gosnold went ashore with a couple dozen men. They liked what they saw. One eyewitness to the site where they came on shore described the land as boasting "faire meddowes and goodly tall Trees, with such Fresh-waters running through the woods as I was almost ravished at the sight thereof."[23] This exploration was interrupted when the local natives "charged us very desperately in the faces."[24] When the colonists opened fire with their crude guns, their assailants scattered back into the woods. Already, violence had broken out between the Englishmen and those who occupied the lands the colonists had just reached.

One of the party's first orders of business after their arrival was to locate a suitable site for their fort. But, before that search began, Captain Newport took care of another bit of important business. The colonists understood that their colony existed under the charter granted to the merchants and investors of the Virginia Company. But the company was located in England. Those investors could not give daily orders as to how the colony should be run. To oversee the decision making, the company men had selected seven colonists to serve on a council in Virginia. The evening following the run-in with the local Native Americans, Newport, who was on the *Susan Constant*, opened a sealed box that contained the list of names of the colony's direct leaders. The list included Newport, Gosnold, Wingfield, and John Ratcliffe. Another was Captain John Martin, son of Sir Richard Martin, Master of the Royal Mint, who had sailed with Francis Drake. Martin had been part of the group that had rescued the survivors of the first Roanoke colony 20 years earlier. The sixth name was Captain George Kendall, whose cousin was a member of Parliament. He had been chosen to write the reports that would be sent back to England. Number seven on the list was Captain John Smith. After all, because Smith was in charge of providing military protection for the colony, it was important that he be involved in other major decisions.

The search for a fort site did not take long. The men explored up the Powhatan River, which they would name after their king as the James River. During the first two weeks of May 1607, the men on the three ships explored the region. They would finally select a site for their settlement. They chose a point of land approximately 30 miles up the James River. There they unloaded their supplies and began work on their new home. They knew they needed to raise a palisade for protection against the local Indian tribes. Their fortifications would also be named after the king: James Fort, or Jamestown.

During the first two weeks of May 1607, the Jamestown colonists searched for a place to establish a fort before settling on a site 30 miles up the James River. The colonists are depicted here constructing the first settlement.

THE FIRST DAYS AT JAMESTOWN

For the first several weeks, life at Fort James advanced slowly but steadily. The Englishmen began to carve their place in the Virginia wilderness. They had left their homes in England behind. But they were intent on creating a New World for England in the frontier lands of North America. The first report sent back to England was positive. "Within less than seven weeks, we are fortified well against the Indians. We have sown good store of wheat. We have sent you a taste of clapboard. We have built some houses."[25] Because the settlement was established as a joint-stock company, the settlers were expected to produce a profit in the New World. The "clapboard" mentioned would have been split oak to be used to make barrels, potentially creating a new industry in Jamestown. But the report also included a call for fresh supplies and more colonists, before the "devouring Spaniard lay his ravenous hands upon these gold-showing mountains."[26]

Gold is exactly what the colony's supporters and stockholders would have wanted the colonists to find. Gold and silver had been found in abundance in the Spanish colonies. The English who dispatched these colonists to Virginia were hoping to discover more of the same. The lure of gold would prove to be a problem for the colony, however. Too many colonists "spent too much time looking for gold and not enough growing crops."[27] It was especially a problem for the "gentlemen" who had come to the New World colony. They were not accustomed to hard work. They thought work was beneath them and was something to be done by commoners. That is how it was in England. But there was no gold to be found in Virginia. The colonists were painting as rosy a picture of their new colony as they could. However, life in Jamestown would prove extremely difficult during not only the early months but also the first years of the colony. The new English settlement along the James River could even be called a death trap.

What would make life so difficult in the Jamestown colony during its earliest years? A number of factors, some the colonists could not control and others of their own making, were responsible. One of the problems was the location of the colony. The island the Englishmen chose did have obvious advantages. It was far enough up the James River so that a raid by a Spanish warship would be difficult. The site could also be easily defended against Native Americans. It was an island, after all, except for a narrow strip or bridge of land at its western

(continues on page 50)

THE NATIVE AMERICANS OF "VIRGINIA," CIRCA 1600

When three English ships arrived along the Atlantic coast in the spring of 1607, they came immediately into contact with the people who were already living on the lands the Englishmen wanted to colonize. They were American Indians. At that time, millions of Native Americans called the lands that would one day become the United States home. Those the Jamestown colonists would settle next to were similar to many others in North America, but their culture was also unique in many ways.

The tribes that lived in the Tidewater region of present-day Virginia and its many rivers belonged to a cultural group called the Algonquins. These tribes lived along the Eastern Atlantic seaboard from modern-day Maine in the north down to what is today Georgia in the south. They spoke many different languages, although they had their roots in an Algonkian dialect. While the specific cultures of each of the dozens of tribes in the region that surrounded Jamestown were different from one another, they also shared important similarities.

The tribes around the English settlement at Jamestown typically lived in small villages, usually home to no more than two- or three-hundred men, women, and children. The villages featured simple huts, small houses built around frames of wooden saplings bent into a round shape and covered over with animal skins, large pieces of tree bark, or reeds woven into sheets or mats. These houses were not meant to be permanent dwellings. Many such villages were abandoned every 5 to 10 years. By then, the villages were worn out, the buildings rotted, the surrounding fields farmed out, and the forests' resources were largely exhausted.

The Native Americans were fishers, farmers, and hunters. The men of each tribe roamed the dense forests in search of large animals, especially deer, for food. Other, smaller animals—including squirrels, rabbits, and beaver—were also hunted. The hides of many different types of animals were used to provide clothing.

While the men hunted and fished, the women usually farmed, planting small fields of pumpkins, as well as corn, squash, and several types of beans. Native Americans referred to this trio of vegetables as "The Three Sisters." But the most important crop grown was corn. It was the main food in their diet. When the wild game were scarce in the winter, whole tribes relied on their stored corn to keep them alive. (The Native Americans grew their beans and corn together in the same fields, so the bean vines could wind around the tall cornstalks.) The women also gathered wild foods, such as berries, fruits, nuts, roots, and other plants.

When not hunting or fishing, the Native American men spent much of their time fighting. War was an important way of life and the primary means by which a young man might prove himself to be brave. Boys were trained for war from an early age. The main weapons used by these warriors included the bow and arrow, as well as many varieties of war clubs. While warriors sometimes killed their enemies in battle, they also took prisoners. Such captives often experienced harsh treatment, with torture a common practice. Prisoners were burned, sometimes one limb at a time. Their limbs were broken and their joints pulled out of their sockets, causing extreme pain. A captive who showed great courage during such cruel treatment might gain the respect of his captors. He might even be adopted by his enemy tribe as an act of honor.

War was so much a part of the culture of the Native Americans who lived on the lands the English settled at Jamestown, that fighting between the tribes and colonists took place repeatedly.

When the colonists established a settlement at Jamestown, they immediately set out to trade with the Native Americans who inhabited the region. Bartholomew Gosnold and other Jamestown settlers are depicted here trading with the Native Americans in an engraving by Theodorus de Bry, which appears in Thomas Harriot's *Brief and True Report of the New Found Land of Virginia.*

(continued from page 47)

end. The nearby woods boasted an abundance of wild game and trees for making timber for houses, as well as for export for profit. A deepwater channel flanked the island that would allow the colonists' ships to be tied up near the settlement. Their cannon could serve as a defense against attack.

But there were also problems with the Jamestown site. Perhaps most importantly, the settlement was established on marshy ground, where countless mosquitoes bred. These mosquitoes spread malaria, a disease that caused an often fatal fever. (In the early 1600s, no one understood that mosquitoes spread malaria.) Also, because Jamestown was built on an island, the groundwater became polluted with human waste, which made the colonists sick, sometimes causing death. As one colonist wrote about the water: "Our drinke [was] cold water taken out of the river, which was at a floud [high tide] verie salt [and] at a low tide full of slime and filth, which was the destruction of many of our men."[28]

Another problem with the Jamestown location was that several Indian tribes lived nearby. An estimated 10,000 to 15,000 people, living in several hundred villages and tribal units, were spread throughout the region surrounding Jamestown, which the Native Americans called Tsenacommacah. Many of these tribes were allied together in the early 1600s as part of the Powhatan Confederacy. Unfortunately for the colonists, the local Native Americans established the confederacy for the purposes of protecting themselves. The Powhatans had powerful enemies to the north, including the Susquehannocks, Mannahoacs, and Massawomecks. Raids and hit-and-run attacks were common between these New World tribes. While Native Americans were, at times, friendly with the newly arrived English colonists, sometimes they chose to attack. Within the Powhatan Confederacy, the Pamunkey was the strongest tribe, with 500 or 600 warriors. The Pamunkeys lived within an easy day's travel of Fort James. This made life difficult for the residents at Jamestown, who grew accustomed to watching over their shoulders every time they ventured outside of their settlement.

6

Trials
and Errors

The Jamestown colonists experienced one of the first con-
frontations with the local Native Americans on May 26, very soon
after selecting the site for their settlement. Edward Maria Wingfield had decided that the colony could be protected by having
the men erect a wall of brush around the site. Soon, he had the
men cutting clapboard, or split oak, instead of logs for a sturdy
palisade. When the Native Americans came, they found many
of the colonists loafing in a field outside their makeshift barrier.
Englishmen scattered and ran as arrows flew. Twelve colonists
were wounded and two later died, including one of the boys.
Only when the cannon on their ships opened fire, sending out a
blast of grapeshot, did the Native Americans retreat. For the moment, Jamestown had survived. But the brush barrier would not.
Captain John Smith had insisted to Wingfield that the men needed to build a strong defensive wall around the settlement, but
Wingfield had ignored him. Over the next two or three weeks, the
Englishmen built a palisade, a true fort. It was built in the shape
of a triangle and at each corner a "Bulwarke" was built, "like a half
Moone and four or five pieces of Artillerie mounted in them."[29]

EXPLORING THE VIRGINIA LANDSCAPE

When Fort James was attacked on May 26, some members of the colony were not present, including John Smith, the man everyone looked to for military protection. Five days earlier, a select number of colonists had boarded the shallop, the small boat, to explore farther upriver. Although Smith did not approve of the exploration (he thought there was much to do at the settlement site), he decided to go, as well. The river trip went reasonably well. The colonists met with friendly Native Americans, who shared food with them, such as deer meat and corn.

Shortly after the settlement site for Jamestown was set up, Captain John Smith led an expedition in this shallop to explore the James River. During the six-day voyage, Smith and his compatriots visited many Native American settlements and established friendly relations with their new neighbors.

The Jamestown settlers traded small gifts such as hawks' bells, small knives, and glass beads.

The voyage up the James River gave the curious colonists an opportunity to see the Native American camps for themselves. They saw their simple houses and how they were built. In many ways, the houses were not much different from the early colonist shelters. They were simple and solid enough to withstand a typical rain- and windstorm. All around these Native American settlements, the Englishmen saw signs of extensive farming, as well as other activities. As one colonist noted:

> They live commonly by the water side in little cottages of canes and reedes, covered with the barke of trees....They live upon sod wheat beanes & peaze for the most part, also they kill deare take fish in their weares [weirs; enclosures in the river for trapping fish], & kill fowle [in] abundance, they eat often and that liberally; they are proper ... men very strong runn exceeding swiftly.[30]

The explorers also saw another type of plant grown by the local tribes. It grew as "a tall, fragrant-flowered herb"[31] and was not eaten but smoked—tobacco. The Virginia tribes grew tobacco for their religious ceremonies. They smoked the plant's dried leaves in reed pipes.

Through the six days of exploration and contact, the Jamestown settlers were able to establish, at least for the moment, friendly relations with the Native Americans whose villages lined the James River, the water highway the colonists relied on just as much as the natives did.

Over the years that followed, the Jamestown colonists lived in close proximity to several tribes, neighbors the Englishmen often found unpredictable. They would establish trade connections with the Native Americans, who often sold beaver hides cheaply, because they did not think beaver skins were really worth anything. The Native Americans would sometimes co-operate with the colonists, helping them plant their first corn crops. As long as the English were able to pacify the leader of the loose confederation of tribes, Powhatan, they could expect friendly relations. Early on, the colonial leaders met with Powhatan and crowned him with a copper crown that had been sent over from England. Between the symbolic "crowning" and the beaver trade, the English and Native Americans often lived peaceably, but the English rarely strayed far from their fort and never without someone bringing along a musket. Unfortunately for the English settlers, this kept them bottled up in their settlement, helping to create an even more unhealthy environment.

JOHN SMITH PROVIDES LEADERSHIP

Among those who led the colonists during Jamestown's early months, none was as important as Captain John Smith. Smith was a hard-nosed, tough leader who knew what the colonists needed to do to survive. Throughout the summer of 1607, the colony struggled even to get by. (By September 10, nearly half of the colonists would be dead, including one of the leaders, Bartholomew Gosnold.) Through the summer and into the fall, houses were not built fast enough, food was scarce, and the colony's gentlemen did not lift a finger and work. Disease spread and, by August 1607, Fort James was home to only five or six healthy colonists. The rest had either died or were sick. Many of the Jamestown settlers turned to Captain Smith for leadership. Smith had fallen out of favor with the colony's leaders early on and had been excluded from many of their plans. But, with the residents of Fort James starving and dying, Smith provided a forceful presence. He put everyone to work, even the gentlemen, telling them, "He that will not worke shall not eate."[32] When Smith found out about a plot among the colonists to abandon the colony for England, he ordered the leader tried for treason and shot. Smith brought a new level of organization to the colony. Tasks that had been left undone for lack of manpower were assigned. Smith "set some to mow, others to binde thatch; some to build houses, others to thatch them . . . so that, in short time, he provided most of them lodgings."[33] Needing food, Smith managed to make an important trade with the Powhatans for corn, a move that probably saved the colony. He set out up the James River and soon came back with his boat "well laden with corn, oysters, fish, and venison."[34] At first, the Powhatans, aware of how desperate the colonists were for food, only offered "handfuls of corn for trade goods,"[35] which Smith declined, insisting on more.

Then, Smith set out in the shallop in search of additional food from the Native Americans. It would prove to be one of his greatest adventures in the New World. Taking the shallop again, he sailed up the Chickahominy River, which flowed north of Jamestown. He made good trades for food with the Native Americans who lived along the river. Several of the tribes he encountered were not part of the Powhatan Confederacy and they wanted to be friends with the white settlers. With each trip, Smith and his companions returned with the shallop full of food, especially corn.

Then, in December, Smith and his associates found themselves in Powhatan territory. They were spotted by unfriendly warriors, who attacked, killing everyone in Smith's small party, except for Smith. He was taken prisoner and carried off to the village of Opechancanough. Many historians believe Opechancanough was the half brother to Chief Powhatan. While in Opechancanough's village, Smith tried to converse with the residents, picking up some of their language. He astonished the Powhatans with a handheld device that featured a small arrow that always pointed north. It was, of course, Smith's compass. Early in his captivity, the Powhatans suddenly tied the English soldier to

(continues on page 58)

THE SOLDIER FROM LINCOLNSHIRE

He is one of the most well-known figures in the early history of English colonization in North America. Yet he is known as much, perhaps, for what he did not do than for what he actually did. Although he was only in his late 20s in 1607, John Smith had a reputation as one of the most experienced soldiers in all of England. It comes as no surprise that he was selected to provide military security for the Jamestown colonists.

He was born on January 9, 1580, in Elizabethan England, the eldest son of a prosperous Lincolnshire farmer. When his father died in 1597, 17-year-old John inherited the family farm. But he would not spend his adult life working the soil. Young John Smith was driven by a sense of adventure. By the time he reached his early 20s, Smith had left home to travel across Europe. By then, he had grown into a young man, short in height even for his time, stocky, sporting a brilliant red beard shaped like a fan. He was already confident and ready to take on the world—literally.

To make his name and increase his fortune, he became a soldier and went to fight the Ottoman Turks, who were menacing central and eastern Europe. He was employed as a mercenary, a soldier of fortune, to fight for the Hungarian prince Zsigmond Báthory. While in the prince's service, young Smith was made a captain.

All did not go well during Smith's military adventures. He was captured in November 1602 during the battle of Rotenturm Pass (in present-day Romania). He was clapped in chains and taken to Constantinople as a prisoner of war, an iron collar around his neck. According to Smith, he was made a slave. In time, he managed to kill his Turkish master and escape (with the help of a beautiful princess). He found his way to Russia, then traveled across Europe through Poland, Germany, France, and Spain. He even landed in northern Africa, only to return to England in 1604. Whether all these events actually took place is not certain. John Smith was a notorious braggart, who may have stretched the truth to make his adventures sound even more exciting than they actually were.

In one of his stories, as two armies faced one another, a Turkish leader named Turbashaw challenged Smith's commander to send out his best soldier to fight him, much like the story of David and Goliath in the Bible. The two combatants charged one another on horseback, each aiming a lance at the other. Smith's lance pierced his enemy, who fell from his horse, dead. Smith then dismounted, took a sword, cut off the man's head, and presented

(continues on next page)

(continued from previous page)

it to his general, "who kindly accepted it."* Two other enemy soldiers then challenged Smith. Each match ended with Smith the victor and his enemy beheaded.

But whether or not he told the truth about all his exploits abroad, when Smith returned to England in 1604, he soon gained a reputation as an experienced soldier. When he heard that a company had been formed to establish a colony in the New World, he was immediately interested. America, after all, represented yet another adventure.

*Bradford Smith, *Captain John Smith: His Life & Legend* (Philadelphia: J.B. Lippincott, 1953), 53.

(continued from page 56)

a tree, notched their arrows in their bowstrings, and prepared to fill Captain Smith full of arrows. But they stopped short. Perhaps they were testing Smith's courage. Smith did not flinch. At Opechancanough's signal, the threatening warriors dropped their bows, untied Smith, and a feast was held that evening, with Smith the apparent guest of honor. Smith remained a prisoner of the Powhatans for a month. Finally, Opechancanough chose not to kill Smith, but delivered him to Chief Powhatan.

MAKING AN AMERICAN LEGEND

The meeting between Captain Smith and the great leader Powhatan took place in a large lodge. The chief's warriors sat along the outer edge of the lodge, while the great chief "sat covered with a great robe made of rarowcun [raccoon] skins, and all the tails hanging by."[36] There were women present, each taking her place behind her husband. At Powhatan's side sat a young girl, perhaps only 11 or 12. She was the chief's daughter Matoaka. She was known by a special name among her father's people, because "her disposition was so lighthearted and lively."[37] The

King Powhatan *comands C.Smith to be slayne* his daughter Pokahontas *beggs his life his thankfullnes and how he Subiected 39 of their kings reade & history*

Although much has been made of the famous tale of Pocahontas saving John Smith from certain death at the hands of her father, Wahunsonacock (Powhatan), modern-day historians interpret the incident differently. According to some, the act may have been designed to show Smith's helplessness; others believe that the ritual was carried out as a way to adopt Smith into the tribe.

young girl was known as "Frolicsome," which, in the language of her people, was the name "Pocahontas." At first, things seemed to be going well between the Powhatan leader and the English soldier. Then, suddenly, a group of warriors rushed forward and grabbed Smith. Captain Smith would write about what happened next:

> Two great stones were brought before Powhatan; then as many as could layd hands on him [Smith], dragged him to them and thereon laid his head . . . [The braves] being ready with their clubs to beat out his brains, Pocahontas, the King's dearest daughter, when no entreaty could prevail, got his head in her arms, and laid her own upon his to save him from death.[38]

The scene Smith describes is, perhaps, the most famous that took place in the history of early Jamestown. But modern historians question whether or not the "rescue" of Smith by Pocahontas actually took place. When he wrote about his encounter with Powhatan the following year in his journal, *True Relation*, Smith did not include the story of Pocahontas laying her head on his to spare his life. He did not tell the story until 1624, when he wrote and published his *Generall Historie of Virginia*.

If the incident actually happened, why did Smith not include it in his writings in 1608? Some historians believe the incident might have occurred, but that Smith misunderstood what was happening. The Powhatans may not have been intent on killing him at all. Instead, the whole scene may have been "staged." The chief may have called for the "ritualistic act designed to demonstrate Smith's helplessness and Powhatan's power."[39] Others interpret the actions as part of the Powhatans' way of adopting Smith into their tribe, especially if they were impressed with Smith's courage. Regardless, Chief Powhatan and his warriors eventually allowed Smith to be set free and return to Jamestown. But he would leave Chief Powhatan's village having made friends with Pocahontas.

7

The Starving Time

When John Smith returned to the English settlement, the situation was even more miserable than when he had left. Winter had set in, bringing further difficulties on the colony. It would be an extremely cold winter in both England and America, one remembered years later as "The Great Frost." By January 1608, only 38 men remained alive out of the 144 who had left England a year earlier. Fortunately, that same month, Captain Newport, who had left the colony to bring back new supplies from England, returned, bringing with him 120 new colonists. Their arrival raised the spirits of the struggling colonists. But just five days after the arrival of the new colonists, a fire "consumed all the buildings of the fort and storehouse of ammunition and provisions."[40] Only three buildings were left standing to house the colonists during the coldest months of the year.

The colonists reached a new level of desperation through the year 1608. However, there was reason for hope. The settlement was at peace with Powhatan's Confederacy. The chief even sent men to teach the colonists how to raise corn and to trap

Upon Captain Christopher Newport's return to Jamestown in January 1608, he discovered that only 38 of the original 144 colonists had survived. Fortunately, during that year, Newport brought nearly 200 new settlers, including the first two women, who are depicted with Newport in this drawing.

fish in weirs. The settlers were able to survive the winter. When spring arrived, Captain Newport sailed back to England. He carried a large amount of ore that he and the colonists hoped contained gold. (Newport would find out it was only mica, a golden-colored mineral that was worthless.) Two months later, another ship, the *Phoenix*, reached Jamestown. Supplies were delivered, and the ship soon left with a cargo of fragrant cedarwood. Captain Smith also sent a manuscript he had written about the colony's first year: *A True Relation of Such Occurrences and Accidents of Noate [Note] as Hath Hapned in Virginia since the First Planting of That Collony*. It would be published in England before year's end.

Captain Newport returned in October with much needed supplies and 70 new settlers, including two women, the first Englishwomen of the colony. (One of the women was not married, but she did not remain single for long.) Among the new arrivals were 28 men who were "gentlemen," and they did not expect to work any more than had those of the original party. Such men did the colony no good, according to Smith. By then, he had been elected as president of the Jamestown council, and his leadership had helped keep the struggling colony from being snuffed out. He wrote a letter back to the London Company's stockholders: "When you send again, I entreat you rather send but thirty Carpenters, husbandmen, gardeners, fishermen, blacksmiths, masons and diggers up of trees, roots, well provided, than a thousand of such as we have."[41] Captain Smith still understood that for Jamestown to survive over the long run it would have to be populated by colonists willing to share in the work and the hardships.

DESPERATE DAYS

The Jamestown colonists experienced extremely difficult times during the first 5 to 10 years following the founding of the colony. Hundreds of colonists died facing the hardships and challenges that included attacks by Native Americans, disease, poor leadership, and bad harvests. But the colony ultimately was able to survive. Perhaps no one deserves more credit for the success of Jamestown after 1610 than two new officials who arrived along the James River the following year—Sir Thomas Dale and Deputy Governor Sir Thomas Gates (who first arrived in Jamestown in 1610). They were sent to Jamestown to get the colonists on their feet and turn the colony into one of productivity, industry, and profit.

In 1609, London Company officials had reached a point of exasperation with the colony. They convinced King James to abolish the old local council government and replace it (through a new charter) with one-man rule, a local governor who could administer Jamestown and its surrounding settlements with a firm hand. The first of these new leaders was "Lord Governor Captain General of Virginia" Thomas West, the third Baron de la Warr (or Delaware). It was Delaware who ordered a fleet of nine ships to Jamestown with fresh supplies. The ships carried 400 new colonists, including women, some of the first sent to the struggling colony. The fleet's commander was Sir Thomas Gates.

During the ocean voyage from England, the ships ran into a violent storm. Seven of the ships managed to get through the tempest and reached Jamestown in August. An eighth ship capsized at sea, and the ninth was beached on Bermuda. Gates was onboard this ship. He and his crew managed to cobble together a pair of smaller vessels from their shipwreck and make their way to Jamestown, arriving the following year on May 20, 1610.

What Gates saw in Jamestown was a nightmare. The colony was in shambles. One of the reasons was that Captain John Smith was no longer the leader of Jamestown.

In the fall of 1609, Smith had been badly burned in a gunpowder explosion. A careless colonist had dropped pipe ash

In 1609, a steady stream of women began arriving in Jamestown. However, even by 1650, when women had been coming to Virginia for more than four decades, men still outnumbered them by as much as four to one.

into Smith's powder flask as the captain lay sleeping on a ship tied 70 miles upriver from Jamestown. The powder had ignited, setting Smith's clothes ablaze. Smith had jumped over the side of the vessel into the water, putting out the flames. But he was badly burned on a 10-inch square of his body. The wounded Smith was taken to the settlement where doctors tried to treat his burns. Nearly half-dead, Smith struggled to recover. But his condition only worsened. On October 3, he was carried on-board the ship, the *Falcon*, to return to England.

Of the 400 colonists Gates had sailed with from England in 1609, plus the settlers who were already living in the colony, only 60 remained alive! The total number of colonists who had come to Jamestown during the first three years of settlement was approximately 600. This means that, by May 1610, nearly 90 percent of the English colonists had died!

The previous winter had been a dreadful one for the young Jamestown colony. Fighting had broken out between the colonists and the Powhatans once again. Powhatan's warriors had kept the colonists pinned down in their settlement fort. They roamed the woods around the English village, keeping the settlers trapped inside the walls of the fort. There was not enough food to keep the colonists alive. The settlers killed and ate anything they could get their hands on. They ate their livestock—including cattle and goats—which they desperately needed for milk. The starving colonists then ate the settlement's dog population, then rodents, including mice and rats. Driven mad by a lack of food, the residents of Jamestown became desperate. They even turned to cannibalism. One colonist described what he saw during that awful winter that would become known as the "Starving Time": "We were constrained [forced] to eat dogs, cats, rats, snakes, toadstools, horsehides, and what not; one man out of the misery endured, killing his wife, powdered [salted] her up to eat her, for which he was burned. Many besides fed on the corpses of dead men."[42] One of the Jamestown colonists became so used to eating human flesh, he developed an appetite for it and had to be executed by his fellow settlers. By the spring of 1610, the population in Fort James had been reduced from nearly 500 residents to 60.

These were some of the darkest days for the Jamestown colony. Everything was in a state of chaos and the colonists were without hope:

> John Smith, injured in a powder explosion, had returned to England the autumn before, and without him the colony had gone to pieces . . . Gates found the palisades gateless and

in ruins, half the houses empty, the chapel fallen into decay. Sickness, lack of food, increasingly bold attacks by the Indians—it was all too much for the leaderless and desperate settlers. They wanted to return to England.[43]

For two weeks following his arrival, Gates tried to keep the colonists from abandoning their outpost settlement. But with little food and sickness everywhere, there was little incentive to remain. On June 10, the remaining ragtag colonists packed up and left Jamestown, setting sail down the James River to return to homes in England many thought they would not live to see again.

NEW HOPE FOR A STRUGGLING COLONY

Despite the adversities the colonists faced, the great English experiment in the Virginia wilderness was not doomed to fail. The colony would not be abandoned. Through a stroke of luck, the weary colonists floating down the James River were met by a fleet of three ships with Lord Delaware himself onboard. The ships carried fresh supplies and 150 new colonists. Delaware ordered Gates to turn his boats around and return to Jamestown. As for the tired and starving colonists, the sight of the three ships was a godsend.

Delaware immediately put the colony back in order. The tumbledown buildings were repaired and better houses constructed. These houses were typical of the kind found in England at the time. They were simply built, half-timbered buildings often measuring little more than twelve-feet wide and six-feet high. The framework was of wooden beams carved out with an English axe. Between the wall beams, braces were added and the spaces between were filled in with material called "wattle-and-daub." The "wattle" was little more than upright wooden sticks woven together. The "daub," a mixture of clay or mud and straw (as a binder) was "plastered" over the wattle, filling in the gaps.

When Lord Delaware (depicted here kneeling) arrived at Jamestown in June 1610, the colonists were on the verge of starvation—by that spring, the population had been reduced from nearly 500 residents to 60. Delaware not only brought fresh supplies and 150 new colonists to Jamestown, but as the new governor of Virginia, he used his administrative talents to put the colony back in order.

Grass "thatch" was used for the roof and a small log and clay chimney was then added. Such houses could be snug, but they also caught fire easily.

Gates also took initiative. He launched a military offensive against the Paspaheghs in August 1610. The attacks were sometimes extremely violent and bloody. The "battle" led to the deaths of 18 Native Americans. Their homes were burned,

(continues on page 72)

JOHN SMITH RETURNS TO AMERICA

The departure of Captain John Smith from the Jamestown colony in the fall of 1609 would have disastrous results for the colonists. Smith had held a prominent role during the colony's first two years, providing important leadership, military knowledge, and the ability to trade with the Native Americans for much-needed food. The gunpowder accident that nearly caused his death was perhaps the worst tragedy to befall the early colony.

Following his departure, Smith was returned to England, where he struggled to recover from his wounds. A determined and strong individual, Smith did return to his former health. For four years, he remained in the land of his birth, publishing a map of the Jamestown colony and searching for another opportunity to return to America. The captain "had seen the new world and he was in love with it."*

But Smith was not drawn to return to Jamestown. He had already explored that region of Virginia. (When the early English colonists referred to "Virginia," they did not mean just the modern-day state. Early seventeenth-century Virginia was all the land along the Atlantic coast from today's South Carolina to the Canadian province of Nova Scotia.) Smith wanted to explore "northern Virginia," the lands he would himself one day name "New England." "As I liked Virginia well," Smith would write, "so I desired also to see this country [New England], and spend some time in trying what I could finde."** By 1614, Smith got his opportunity.

Smith had heard of New England from Bartholomew Gosnold, one of the important leaders in early Jamestown. (Gosnold had died that first summer on August 22, 1607.) Gosnold had made an earlier voyage to New England, exploring from Nova Scotia to modern-day Massachusetts. It was Gosnold who had named such Massachusetts locations as Cape Cod and Martha's Vineyard. Gosnold had come away from his time in New England much impressed with the fertility of the land and the abundance of fish and other seafood in the region.

The eager and fully recovered captain found four London merchants willing to finance a small party to New England, including two ships. In the spring of 1614, Smith and his party set sail down the Thames on March 3. Onboard one of the ships was an American Indian named Squanto, who had been taken by English fishermen several years earlier from his home in New England. Smith had met Squanto and promised to return to his

(continues on next page)

(continued from previous page)

village on Cape Cod. (Six years later, Squanto would be one of the Native Americans who greeted the arrival of another English ship filled with colonists—the *Mayflower*.)

After several weeks at sea, the two English vessels reached Monhegan Island off the coast of modern-day Maine, opposite the mouth of the Kennebec River. The site was a common docking point for English fishermen. During the annual fishing season, as many as 200 ships might be seen in the waters around Monhegan Island. One of the first activities Smith and his men engaged in was whale hunting. While they saw many whales in the region's waters, they were unable to kill any of them. It would be the first disappointment for Smith and his newly arrived group of English adventurers.

In the fall of 1609, John Smith was badly burned by a gunpowder explosion and had to return to England for treatment. During his time in England, he published this map, which details the area around the Jamestown colony.

Smith's next endeavor was to search for gold. However, much like the area around Jamestown, New England was devoid of the valuable mineral. Smith then turned his interest to other potential sources of trade and wealth in the region—fish and fur. Unfortunately, he and his men had spent so much time chasing whales that the season for harvesting either animal had already passed. In Smith's words: "The prime of both those seasons were past ere wee perceived it."*** While the men managed to harvest 50,000 pounds of fish by the end of the summer, it was not enough to cover the investment of their London sponsors.

Even as most of Smith's men spent months fishing, he and eight or nine others spent their time exploring. This was Smith's true calling. He loved the search that led him up new rivers and water inlets. He was especially skillful at making maps. (As Smith explored and mapped, his small party trapped for furs, collecting more than 1,000 beaver pelts and 100 otter skins.) For weeks, Smith explored along the coast of modern-day Maine and Massachusetts. One of the places he was most impressed with was a great bay that could be used as a harbor for ships. It would later be the site of Boston. A similar harbor site was Plymouth, where the Pilgrims would land just over six years later.

During his explorations, Smith and his men came into contact with the local Native Americans. Since they spoke a language similar to that spoken by the Powhatans near Jamestown, Smith was able to talk with them, as he described later, "in a broken language."† Everywhere Smith went, he became more excited about what he saw. New England was a rich region, filled with fur-bearing wildlife, endless forests, clear streams, abundant plant life, and sea waters teeming with fish, shell food, and lobster. Smith decided that any future colonization in New England would be based on fishing. The captain was convinced that "the 'silver streames' of fish were New England's answer to the gold of Spanish America."†† By mid-July, Smith and his men were ready to return home to England. Although one of the ships remained in the region a bit longer, Smith's ship was soon on its way back across the Atlantic loaded with furs, salted fish, and a large supply of fish oil.

---

* Bradford Smith, *Captain John Smith: His Life & Legend* (Philadelphia: J.B. Lippincott, 1953), 186.

**Ibid.

***Ibid., 191.

†Ibid., 196.

††Ibid.

(continued from page 68)

the cornfields were cut down, and the Paspahegh chief's children were brutally killed. One eyewitness described their murders as "effected by Throweinge them overboard and shoteinge out their Braynes in the water."[44] The colonists almost burned the chief's wife at the stake. But they were stopped by one of the party's captains, who convinced them to put her to death with a sword instead. (The Native Americans thought this was a more humane way to kill someone than burning.) Such fighting continued through the following year. Dozens of colonists were killed when the Paspaheghs launched harsh attacks of their own.

As for Delaware, he did not remain in the colony even a year. Following his departure in March 1611, the next leader at Jamestown was Deputy Governor Sir Thomas Dale, who had military experience. He arrived in Jamestown the following May. While Delaware had managed to get the Jamestown colonists back on their feet, it would be Governor Dale who would rally the colony to greater success.

8

A Future in Tobacco

Thomas Dale would soon become Jamestown's new John Smith. He and Gates established something very close to military rule, because of the dire conditions in the colony. The colonists had slipped into old habits following Delaware's departure. Dale found a colony where the corn crop had not yet been planted and "most of the companie were at their daily and usually workes, bowling in the streets."[45] Immediately he clamped down, establishing a strict set of rules for the colonists, called "Dale's Laws." (Delaware and Gates had already established the "Civill and Politique Laws," but Dale added to them.) In these laws, Dale told the colonists what he expected of them, especially when it came to work. Nearly everyone was required to work the colony's fields from 6 to 10 in the morning and 2 to 4 in the afternoon. The remainder of their time could be spent working in their own gardens and repairing their houses, pens, and fences. The punishments for breaking these rules were harsh: They included hanging, prison, and burnings. When some colonists stole food from the fort's supplies, they were "[bound] faste unto Trees and so [starved] them to deathe."[46]

DALE TAKES CONTROL

Change was soon the norm at Jamestown. For one thing, the Jamestown settlement site was moved 50 miles farther inland to get away from the unhealthy swamps. To encourage the settlers to do more work, Dale changed the land policy of the colony. Previously, all the land used for farming was worked by everyone. No one owned his own property. This often led to some of the settlers being lazy. Those who now worked the hardest were given some small pieces of land of their own. Here they could grow some additional food for themselves. The plan worked. Soon, food production increased dramatically. There were so many people working their little private plots of land that the fort had to be enlarged.

This led Dale to look around for other sites where the colonists could expand, away from the swampy site at Jamestown. He soon located one upriver on the James, where the river made a sharp curve. Dale selected one of the peninsulas of land along this part of the river and named it Henrico, after Henry, Prince of Wales. A group of settlers made Henrico their home, and it was soon the site of 50 houses and a church. The colonists built blockhouses that would easily protect them from attack. Dale then had another protective fort built about 10 miles farther upriver, along the Falls of the Appomattox River. The new site was called "Bermuda Hundred," after the island Gates and others had washed up on. ("Hundred" was an old English legal term for a political district.) Away from the swamps of Jamestown, new groups of colonists were able to live safely and in good health. They grew their own food and increased in numbers. At these new locations, English colonists managed to "strengthen their feeble, by-the-fingertips grasp of a piece of the New World."[47]

THE GOLDEN WEED

Through the decades following 1611, Jamestown's residents created a world for themselves that would bring success to the colony and even a profit for its investors. At the center of those profits was the introduction of a single crop to the fields surrounding Jamestown—tobacco.

The man responsible for making tobacco a cash crop was Master John Rolfe, who had arrived in the Jamestown colony along with Gates. He was a gentleman, the son of a Norfolkshire squire. Tobacco was grown in Virginia by the Powhatans when the English colonists arrived, but the Indian tobacco (*Nicotiana rustica*) was not popular with the English. Back in England, Englishmen loved their tobacco. It had reached the Old World through Christopher Columbus and had quickly spread across Europe. The popular way to enjoy tobacco was by smoking it in clay pipes, which were cheap, making it possible for nearly anyone to afford one. (In English taverns, clay pipes were hung on the walls to be used by customers.)

But tobacco was expensive. Most was imported through the Caribbean and sold in England for as much as 18 shillings a pound. This was nearly a month's wages for a common English worker! As for the tobacco the Jamestown colonists found in Virginia, it had a strong, even harsh taste. There was no point in raising it for exportation. It would not be popular back in England.

It was Rolfe who put two and two together. In 1611, he bought some tobacco seeds from Trinidad, an island in the Caribbean, and Venezuela in South America, where tobacco was grown. He began experimenting with growing this milder variety of tobacco (*Nicotiana tabacum*) on Virginia soil. The plants grew well. Then, Rolfe tried different methods of "curing," or drying the brown tobacco leaves. After two years, he sent a supply of his hybrid Virginia tobacco to some English importers. It met their approval. Now, Virginia-produced tobacco could be sold in England, and the profits would help the colony turn yet another corner. Also, by 1613, the Virginia Company was assigning three-acre plots of land to each colonist. This new combination of land and crop became a common sight in the

(continues on page 78)

JOHN ROLFE AND POCAHONTAS

History tells the modern reader about such important Virginia residents as Pocahontas and of the Englishman who made tobacco profitable in Jamestown. Each made their individual contribution to Virginia history and that of the English settlement. But the paths of both the American Indian maiden and the English gentleman from Norfolkshire would cross in the New World. Their story is one of both love and tragedy.

In the spring of 1613, just as tobacco was starting to become a success in Jamestown, the colonists faced a series of raids by the Powhatans. In one counterraid, a ship's captain for the London Company managed to capture Pocahontas, then a young woman of 18. She was held in Jamestown for a year. Governor Dale demanded that Pocahontas's father pay a

In 1614, Pocahontas, the daughter of Wahunsonacock (Powhatan), married John Rolfe, who helped teach her the ways of the English after she had been captured during a raid against the Powhatans. In 1616, the couple traveled to England, where they visited the royal court of King James.

ransom that included the return of "several runaway Englishmen, certain stolen tools and firearms, together with 500 bushels of corn."* Although she would later be released, Pocahontas, while in Jamestown, learned the ways of the English, including common customs and manners. She was also introduced to Christianity and agreed to be baptized. One of the colonists who taught her about her new faith was John Rolfe.

While teaching Pocahontas, it seems Rolfe fell in love with her, and she with him. Rolfe then asked permission from Governor Dale for the two to marry. He agreed. Pocahontas also contacted her father and he, too, agreed. Powhatan sent two of Pocahontas's brothers and an uncle to represent him at the wedding, which was held in April 1614. Pocahontas, in becoming the wife of an Englishman, took on a new name, Rebecca. The English colonists and Powhatan's people seemed to think the marriage of Rolfe and Pocahontas was a sign that the two peoples should agree to get along. Over the next few years, there would be no fighting between the English and the people of Powhatan.

The marriage seemed to be a good one for both bride and groom. Pocahontas, in time, gave birth to a son named Thomas. But all did not remain well. John Rolfe took his wife to England in 1616. There she was presented to the royal court, dressed in the Englishwomen's fashion of the day. The intriguing Indian woman was well received. (There were some members of the Royal Court who did not approve of the marriage. They considered Rolfe little more than a commoner, whereas Pocahontas was an Indian princess.) Then, tragedy struck. When the Rolfe family prepared to board a ship to return to the land they both called home, Pocahontas became ill with smallpox. The disease was deadly, and outbreaks were common during this time. Pocahontas lived only a few days with the disease, then died. Ironically, perhaps, just two years later, Powhatan, her father, died, probably of a plague introduced to the New World by the Europeans.

As for her son, Thomas, his father, John, decided to leave him in England to be raised and educated. But, when he was a young man, Thomas left England and returned to America. There, he prospered and his descendants became one of the important families of Virginia.

---

*Carl Bridenbaugh, *Jamestown, 1544–1699* (New York: Oxford University Press, 1980), 22.

(continued from page 75)

colony. Over the next three years, hundreds of Jamestown colonists were growing tobacco. In Jamestown proper, "the golden weed grew in the streets"[48] when the colonists ran out of available land. Tobacco became the new success story for the Virginia colonists. In London, tobacco fetched a price that was six times that of wheat.

Growing tobacco became the mainstay of the Jamestown colony's economy. So many settlers began growing the smoking weed that Sir Thomas Dale had to remind them to plant some of their fields with corn and other crops or they would starve. However, tobacco was very profitable. For example, in 1617, a merchant ship, the *George,* delivered a cargo of 20,000 pounds of Virginia tobacco to England. There, it sold for more than five shillings a pound. The London Company, as well as those who planted and harvested the golden leaves of tobacco, all made a quick fortune. The company began to promote its colony's tobacco, and the crop soon became very profitable. By 1618, the colony was able to produce almost 50,000 pounds of tobacco. This crop boon also led to an increase in the population in Jamestown.

In many ways, the introduction of tobacco to the colony of Virginia changed life for the colonists more than anything else. It not only produced profits, but it served as a type of money in Virginia. Colonists paid their taxes in tobacco. Public servants, soldiers, government workers, even preachers were paid with the profitable plant. For the rest of the eighteenth century, tobacco was the chief export of the region. By the time of the start of the American Revolution in the 1770s, colonists were exporting 50 million pounds of tobacco each year. The two colonies that were dominating the tobacco market in America by the eighteenth century were Virginia and its neighbor to the north—Maryland.

Indentured servants, such as the woman depicted in this engraving, traveled to Virginia in large numbers when tobacco became an important cash crop in the mid-1600s. After working for their masters for four to seven years, indentured servants were free to strike out on their own.

NEW WORKERS NEEDED

There were problems with growing tobacco in abundance, however. Sometimes colonists grew too much tobacco, more than people wanted to buy. This drove the price down, hurting each farmer's profits. Tobacco was also hard on the soil. Colonists did not fertilize their fields in the 1600s. The tobacco plants sapped the nutrients from the soil, causing the land to wear out in only four to seven years. This caused farmers and plantation

POPULATION GROWTH IN EARLY JAMESTOWN AND VIRGINIA

Just over 100 male colonists arrived along the James River in the spring of 1607 to establish the Jamestown colony. Over the following generation, thousands of English people—men, women, and children—followed, reaching the small English colony as new settlers. But the growth of Jamestown and Virginia in general was not steady through many of those years. There were ups and downs, which meant that many of those who reached the colony did not survive. The following chronology marks the rise and fall of the number of English colonists who struggled to survive in Jamestown and Virginia.

DATE	POPULATION
May 1607	104 (first landing of colonists)
Early January 1608	38 (death from disease and Indian attacks)
October 1608	200 (from new arrivals)
Summer 1609	131 (death from disease)
August 1609	381 (from new arrivals)
October 1609	280 (death from Indian attacks)
May 1610	90 ("Starving Time")
June 1610	375 (from new arrivals)
December 1610	250 (death from disease and Indian attacks)
Late March 1611	152 (departures; death from Indian attacks)
Early May 1611	482 (from new arrivals)
August 1611	752 (from new arrivals)
December 1611	600 (death from Indian attacks)
May 1615	400
1619	700 (approximate)
1619–22	Governor Sandys sends out 3,570 settlers
1622 (before Indian attack)	1,240
1625	1,300
1626	2,600
1627	3,200
1634	5,200
1644	8,000

*Source: Statistics from J. Frederick Fausz, "An 'Abundance of Blood Shed on Both Sides': England's First Indian War, 1609–1614," *Virginia Magazine of History and Biography*, 98 (1990), 55–56; and Edmund S. Morgan, *American Slavery, American Freedom: The Ordeal of Colonial Virginia* (New York: W.W. Norton & Company, 1975), 404.

owners to have to purchase new lands for tobacco cultivation. Sometimes they would have to move to completely new lands. This, then, caused settlement to grow throughout Virginia.

Tobacco also had an impact on the labor force. Growing the crop required lots of work. Tobacco plants were easily damaged by weeds. This meant that the tobacco had to be hoed often, which was difficult, backbreaking work. (The work became known as "chopping tobacco.") So much tobacco was grown, especially after 1650, that it caused a labor shortage in Virginia. This led to the introduction of two new types of workers. One was black laborers. They were brought to the colony from Africa. But the number of black workers did not dramatically increase in Virginia until after the 1670s or so.

In earlier decades, another labor force was used—indentured servants. An indentured servant was a colonist who was too poor to pay his or her ship passage to America. Instead, a wealthy colonist paid for the voyage, leaving the new arrival with a debt. He or she signed a contract, called an indenture. This required the new English immigrant to work for his or her master for a period typically between four and seven years to pay off the debt. During the indenture period, these servants or workers were not allowed to marry. They worked, lived on the master's property, and were provided food, clothing, and shelter. Once the period of indenture was over, the worker received, from the master, his "freedom dues," which might include a new suit of clothes, some farming tools, seeds to plant, and perhaps a small amount of money. Once they were free, such workers could live wherever they wanted in the colony. Between 1625 and 1640, approximately 1,000 indentured servants reached the Tidewater region each year. Once they were free, they often moved farther up Virginia's rivers, seeking land of their own.

After more women were brought to the colony in 1619, marriages took place, and children became more common in the English colony. For decades, however, the number of men remained higher than the number of women. Even as late as 1650, men outnumbered women at Jamestown by three or four to one. Only by about 1700 would the number of women be equal to the number of men.

9

The End of an Era

With the difficulties seemingly over—including shortage of food, poor leadership, a lack of direction, and raids by Native Americans—Jamestown became the New World destination for thousands. Between 1619 and 1625, more than 4,000 English colonists flocked to make their homes and fortunes in Virginia. Even wealthier colonists began to arrive. By company policy, any English merchant or skilled craftsman who could afford to pay ship passage for himself, his spouse, and a single male child would be granted title to 150 acres of Virginia land. This amount of acreage was large compared to land in England. That same immigrant and his family could also buy additional land at a reduced rate.

EDWIN SANDYS TAKES CONTROL

With each passing year, the lure to Virginia became greater. In 1619, Sir Edwin Sandys gained leadership and control of the London Company. He immediately changed the colony's leadership, replacing the hardline rule of Governor Dale with another

In 1619, the Dutch ship *Jesus of Lubeck* arrived at Jamestown with 20 blacks who had been purchased in West Africa. At the time, slavery did not exist in Virginia, but the Jamestown colonists welcomed the newcomers and employed them in the cultivation of their tobacco fields.

leader who was less strict—Sir George Yeardley. That same year, Virginians gained the right to elect some of their own leaders. Yeardley had arrived in Virginia with orders to set up a general assembly. The political body was to have two houses. The Upper House would serve as the governor's council. The Lower House would consist of 11 "burroughs," or districts, each with its own representative. The whole idea was similar to the English Parliament in London. It was called the House of Burgesses. (A "burgess" was a representative for people living in a certain region of the colony.) The body's purpose was to "make and ordaine whatsoever lawes and orders should by them be thought good and proffitable."[49] The House of Burgesses met for the first time in the summer of 1619 in the Jamestown church. At its first meeting, the burgesses passed laws against gambling, public drunkenness, swearing, and laziness.

That same year, another important change was introduced to the Jamestown colony and Virginia in general. A Dutch ship arrived one day, the *Jesus of Lubeck*, with passengers from Africa. The ship's captain unloaded 20 blacks who had been purchased along the west coast of Africa. If these blacks had been taken to the Caribbean instead of Virginia, they would have been sold as slaves. But slavery did not exist in Virginia or by English law, so these blacks simply became a part of the workforce in Jamestown and at plantations up and down the river. (There were, in fact, 22 blacks who had already reached Jamestown earlier that same year.) The colonists were only too happy to take these new arrivals off the hands of the Dutch traders. The Virginia residents needed more workers to cultivate their fields of tobacco.

LOOKING BACK ON THE COLONY

The previous 12 years of colonization had taken their toll on the English who had made their way to America. During that period, more than 6,000 English colonists—men, women, and children—had reached the banks of the James River to make new homes for themselves. By 1619, approximately 700 of those colonists were still alive. Living in Virginia was still a risky proposition. Even after the days when the harshest problems of early Jamestown had come to an end, succeeding in the colony was still a challenge.

The following year, the colonists in Virginia were joined in the New World by a group of new English colonists. In 1620, a ship named the *Mayflower* reached the Atlantic shores to the north of the colony on the Chesapeake. At the site of modern-day Massachusetts, just over 100 English colonists, now often called the Pilgrims, landed at a place they would call Plymouth. Many of them had chosen to come to America for religious reasons. When this new group of immigrants left England, they were bound for Virginia and the Jamestown colony. But a violent storm had blown them to the north, off course by hundreds of miles. When they realized they had landed in the wrong place, they decided to remain there. They would never become Virginia colonists.

During the first 15 years of English settlement at Jamestown, the Native Americans never managed to destroy the colony. However, they never intended to destroy the colony, just limit its expansion. But, by the early 1620s, Chief Powhatan was dead, killed by an epidemic that swept up and down the Atlantic coast. At his death, Opechancanough became the new leader of the Powhatans. He did not like the presence of English colonists on his lands and was determined to drive them off. In 1622, he and his warriors attacked English settlements along the James River. Opechancanough had never tolerated the presence of whites on the Powhatans' lands. For years, the English had settled wherever they felt safe, had cut down endless acres of timber, had killed the wildlife, and built permanent homes with no intentions of leaving. The new Powhatan Confederacy chief planned a series of well-coordinated attacks on at least 80 locations where white settlers lived. To make certain that the English would not suspect anything, he sent a special message to Jamestown, reminding the colonists of the peace that existed between them and his people. He stated that the peace was so secure that the sky "should sooner fall than it dissolve."[50]

Then, in the early morning hours of Good Friday, March 22, 1622, just weeks short of the fifteenth anniversary of the founding of Jamestown, his warriors attacked up and down the rivers of Virginia and throughout the countryside. Soon, more than 300 colonists came under the knives of the Powhatans, including women and children. It was a brutal attack:

> They caught farmers preparing tobacco patches, workmen making brick, carpenters sawing, housewives at their chores, and killed them with clubs or arrows before they could get to their matchlocks [guns] . . . In some places the Indians came into English houses as though to trade or share breakfast, as they were accustomed to do, and then dispatched the family with their own tools. In their unleashed fury, the warriors sometimes hacked and chopped at the corpses of their victims long after death.[51]

Fortunately, Opechancanough did not follow up these brutal attacks to completely destroy the English settlements. He believed that his initial assaults would cause the English to give up and leave Virginia altogether. But he was wrong. Colonists, instead, began to carry out attacks of their own. They raided Native American villages, killing their inhabitants, stealing their foodstores, and burning their "little cottages of canes and reedes."[52] The English attacks continued off and on for the next two years. During the summer of 1624, a small army of 60 well-armed Englishmen, most wearing chest armor, sailed up the James and were soon met by a party of nearly 800 Native American warriors. A two-day battle followed. The Native

Americans' arrows were not able to penetrate the colonists' armor. Many Powhatans were either killed or wounded. On the English side, there were no deaths and only 16 men wounded.

This bloody July battle had far-reaching results. It broke the Powhatan Confederacy forever. The battle showed the Native Americans that they could not defeat well-armed Englishmen. There would be other fights over the years between Native Americans and English colonists in Virginia. But the day had long passed when the Native Americans could have successfully destroyed the English toehold in the New World. The numbers of Native Americans in Virginia were also declining. In 1607—the year the Jamestown colony was established by just over 100 settlers—Virginia was home to at least 10,000 Native Americans. As the years passed, thousands of new colonists arrived. In the meantime, Native American numbers decreased. By 1670, Virginia, including Jamestown, was home to approximately 30,000 white residents, while Native Americans numbered only 6,000! What had happened to 4,000 Native Americans? Some had died of European diseases. Others had been starved out of existence. Still others understood that their lives were threatened by the English and chose to move farther west to get away.

NEW TURNING POINTS

While Jamestown and its outlying colonial settlements would survive the Massacre of 1622, the colony would soon face an important turning point. The massacres caused King James I to forever alter the future of Jamestown. James had never been a supporter of the efforts of the London Company. He believed their governing council was too liberal in how it ran the colony. There were also members of the council who were members of Parliament, who were beginning to challenge the rule of James and the Stuart family. With constant reports of conflicts between the English and Native Americans, plus other ongoing problems, James decided to take bold steps. He blamed the

London Company, stating that company officials had "failed to supply and defend its colonists adequately."[53] Alarmed, London Company officials delivered a petition to Parliament, asking for support. But the king would have his way. On May 24, 1624, King James revoked the original charter of the London Company, stripping Virginia from its control. From that date forward, Jamestown, Henrico, Bermuda Hundred, and all the other English settlement sites in the Tidewater region would exist as part of a royal colony.

When James I died suddenly a year later, some wondered if Virginia would be returned back to the London Company. But it was not to be. The new monarch, James's son Charles I, was just as determined to keep the Tidewater region under the royal thumb. The government of Virginia, he announced, would "immediately depend upon Our Selfe, and not be committed to any Company or Corporation."[54] However, the change from company colony to royal dominion would not mark the end of growth in Jamestown and Virginia.

By 1625, the Massacre of 1622 was a mere memory. The colony continued to thrive with tobacco still its main export. A count of the English colonists in Virginia set the non-native population at approximately 1,300. These colonists, the latest to brave the difficulties of the New World, lived in 21 settlements, scattered along the James River and the Eastern Shore. As for Jamestown, its population was 125 individuals. Near the fort and town was another settlement called "New Towne," which an additional 212 colonists called home. (This settlement site had been laid out just a few years earlier.) New Towne was thriving, "a cluster of private dwelling, storehouses, and workshops where wealthy merchants, artisans, and public officials lived and worked."[55] Jamestown and its surrounding "suburbs" were still a frontier settlement, but it was "beginning to [look like] an urban community," where its English residents could "enjoy their healths and lives as plentifully as in any parte of England."[56]

Despite all its earlier problems, the Jamestown colony managed to survive. By the 1620s, colonists had fanned out up and down the James River, establishing additional settlements and plantations. Tobacco was introduced, providing a cash crop that produced a profit. A representative government was established, the House of Burgesses. Blacks were introduced to the colony to provide additional workers. All these became part of colonial life in Jamestown and Virginia for the generations that followed.

A PROSPEROUS COLONY

The same year—1624—that King James I cancelled the Virginia Company's charter and turned Virginia into a royal colony, Captain John Smith published a new history of Jamestown and the colony of Virginia. He knew that the collapse of the company marked an important change for the region around Jamestown. He wanted to be the one to write about the years of Jamestown's founding and early settlement. Smith called his history, *The Generall Historie of Virginia, New-England, and the Summer Isles*. It was written in six parts, one describing the English settlement in Bermuda, a second on New England, and the remaining four on Virginia. As Smith wrote, he described how important Jamestown, Virginia, and the New World settlements (as noted in the sidebar on pages 69 to 71, Smith had returned to America and led an expedition north of Virginia into the region that would become known as New England) he had helped establish were to him. He described them as "my children . . . my wife, my Hawks, Hounds, my Cards, my Dice, and in totall, my best content."[57] There could be no question from his words that America held a special place for Captain John Smith.

But in his history, Smith was uncertain whether or not the English settlements in America would survive over the long run. He insisted that Virginia could remain a vital part of the English colonial empire, but only if it continued as a productive colony, one that traded its domestic goods around the world. Only then would the future of Jamestown and the other English settlements hugging the Atlantic coast continue and prosper.

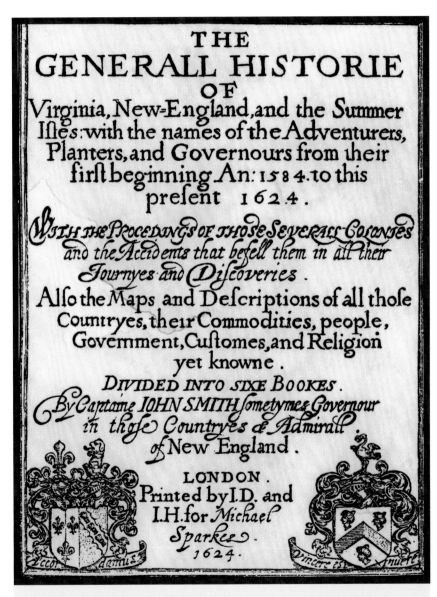

In 1624, John Smith published *The Generall Historie of Virginia, New-England, and the Summer Isles*, which was an account of his time in Jamestown and the colony of Virginia. This woodcut is of the book's title page.

As for Smith's prediction about the future survival of Virginia, he would be proven correct. Trade would be the salvation of the colony. Over the following decades leading up to the turn of the century, the colony continued to grow. First dozens, then hundreds of English trade ships sailed in and out of the Tidewater region, delivering the endless bounty, especially tobacco, of New World farms and plantations. As early as 1640, imports of tobacco to England reached 1 million pounds. By 1670, it had increased to 15 million pounds and nearly doubled again by the turn of the century. Success would be the final chapter for the English who colonized in America.

However, their success would extend far beyond the shores of the Tidewater or the James River. During John Smith's lifetime, the number of English colonists in Virginia and Bermuda combined was never greater than 5,000. But by 1680, the English colonies stretching along the Atlantic seaboard, including Virginia, were home to 150,000 Europeans, the vast majority of whom were English. Throughout the 1600s, the century of Jamestown's founding, 125,000 colonists reached the Chesapeake region. The history of the region would be a story filled with adventure, heartbreak, struggle, starvation, and an enduring spirit of colonization. The legacy of Jamestown would be clear, for it would be on a small island in a river named for an English monarch that the great English experiment on the American frontier would be first planted, then grow, then prosper, then flourish.

THE FINAL DAYS FOR JAMESTOWN

With the decision made by King James I in 1624 to dissolve the Virginia Company and turn Virginia into a royal colony, the history of the colony, including Jamestown, changed forever. By creating a royal colony, the king had destroyed the government of Virginia, including the House of Burgesses. This important legislative body was dissolved until 1639, when Charles I, James's son, reestablished it. In fact, from the 1630s until 1660, the colony of Virginia was largely left to rule itself. During those decades, England struggled with a civil war at home (which ended in 1649 with the beheading of Charles I) and Puritan rule in England at the hands of Oliver Cromwell and his son.

By 1675, Jamestown had grown further and its future as an important colonial town for the 1700s looked bright. But it was not to be. Jamestown would never grow into a thriving colonial capital like those settlements in other colonies, such as Boston, New York, or Newport. The following year, Jamestown was burned by a rebel party of discontented Virginians who were protesting the Virginia governor's slow responses to attacks by Native Americans on the Virginia frontier. Thirty years later, after a generation of recovery, Jamestown had not regained its former prestige. As one resident described things: "This unhappy town did never after arrive at the perfection it then had."[58]

One problem that had plagued Jamestown in earlier decades did not continue after the 1640s. Almost from the first day the original Jamestown colonists reached the shores of the James River, clashes with Native Americans had taken place over and over again. The Massacre of 1622 had been so severe that hundreds of colonists had been killed, and King James had finally decided to take the colony from its founding joint-stock company.

But through the remainder of the 1620s and the 1630s, as more English settlers poured into the region of the James River and its neighboring rivers, the Native Americans were eventually outnumbered. Some of the tribes that had lived in the region for hundreds of years chose to leave and move elsewhere to avoid the destruction of their tribal ways. Chief Opechancanough did manage to launch another series of attacks in 1644, which brought the deaths of 400 colonists. But it would be his last. He was taken prisoner and delivered to a filthy Jamestown jail. Nearly 100 years old, worn out with age and weary struggle, Opechancanough died in prison in 1646, shot by one of his English guards.

Even as some Native Americans packed up and left their tribal lands surrounding Jamestown, another group was increasing in numbers. Prior to the 1650s, the blacks who lived in Virginia were typically workers, like indentured servants, who served their masters for a limited number of years, and were then set free. But, by the 1660s and '70s, Virginia laws were written to define blacks as permanent slaves. Over the following decades, the number of black slaves delivered to Jamestown and other Virginia settlements increased dramatically. By 1750, black slaves numbered more than 100,000, nearly half the colony's population.

With the burning of Jamestown in the 1670s, the next 20 years would finally seal its fate. The town remained the capital into the 1690s. But other events would work against Jamestown. By 1689, the House of Burgesses began considering opening the first college in Virginia. When looking for a site for the college, an important colonist, Colonel John Page, offered part of his lands, called Middle Plantation, for the planned educational institution. Middle Plantation was located between the James and York Rivers, several miles from Jamestown. The Burgesses agreed, and a charter was granted by King William. In 1695, construction began on a college that would be named for the English monarch and his queen—the College of William and Mary. The college opened in 1698.

That same year, events moved in unison to seal Jamestown's future. On October 31, 1698, Jamestown was engulfed in yet another fire. While Jamestown had been rebuilt after the earlier fire in the 1670s, the town had never regained its former prestige or population. A suggestion was made to move the capital to Middle Plantation, near the site of the just opened College of William and Mary. The following April, the General Assembly of

In September 1676, Nathaniel Bacon (depicted here) burned Jamestown to the ground in protest to Governor William Berkeley's friendly policies toward Native Americans. Over the next couple of decades, Jamestown's influence began to fade, and in 1699, Williamsburg became the new capital of the colony of Virginia.

the House of Burgesses agreed. Jamestown, where English colonization had begun nearly a century earlier, soon became an unimportant Virginia community. The new capital, like its new college, would be named for the English monarch—Williamsburg.

Chronology

1492 Sailing on behalf of the Spanish monarchy, Genoese seaman Christopher Columbus reaches the New World, opening the Western Hemisphere to European colonization.

1496 England's King Henry VII sends Genoese seaman John Cabot to explore the northern coast of the New World.

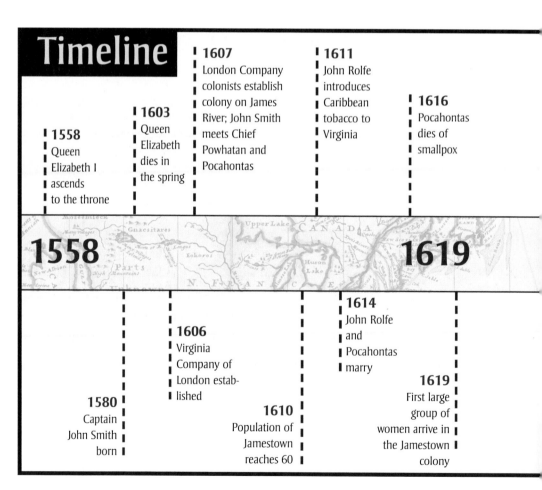

Timeline

1558
Queen Elizabeth I ascends to the throne

1603
Queen Elizabeth dies in the spring

1607
London Company colonists establish colony on James River; John Smith meets Chief Powhatan and Pocahontas

1611
John Rolfe introduces Caribbean tobacco to Virginia

1616
Pocahontas dies of smallpox

1558

1619

1580
Captain John Smith born

1606
Virginia Company of London established

1610
Population of Jamestown reaches 60

1614
John Rolfe and Pocahontas marry

1619
First large group of women arrive in the Jamestown colony

1501 Henry VII sends company of ships bearing English and Portuguese merchants to Newfoundland in modern-day Canada.

1500s The Spanish Empire dominates colonization in the Americas.

1558 Queen Elizabeth I ascends to the English throne.

1577 Queen Elizabeth I sends "sea dog" Francis Drake to engage in raids against Spanish treasure ships in the Caribbean.

1580 Captain John Smith is born.

1580s English sea captains and adventurers begin challenging Spanish power in the New World by expanding English trade.

1622 Chief Opechancanough launches a series of attacks that kill 300 colonists

1625–1640 Approximately 1,000 indentured servants reach the Tidewater region each year

1646 Chief Opechancanough dies

1699 Jamestown abandoned as the capital of Virginia

1676 Jamestown is burned by discontented Virginians

1620

1699

1624 John Smith publishes his *Generall Historie of Virginia*

1640 Tobacco exports from Virginia to England reach 1 million pounds

1660s–1670s Blacks defined as permanent slaves

1583 Englishman Sir Humphrey Gilbert reaches Newfoundland to establish New World trade colony; his efforts fail.

1584 Following Gilbert's death at sea, Elizabeth grants right to colonize in New World to his half brother, Sir Walter Ralegh; that summer, Ralegh sends group to search for New World colonial site.

1585 Ralegh sends colonists to settle on Roanoke Island off the coast of modern-day North Carolina.

1586 Ralegh's Roanoke Colony fails; he begins plans for a second colony.

1587 Ralegh sends second group of colonists to Roanoke.

1588 King Philip II of Spain sends his navy to England to conquer the island empire; the English defeat Philip's "Spanish Armada."

1590 The second colony at Roanoke vanishes; no permanent English colony in North America has yet been founded.

1602 English adventurers and merchants establish Popham Colony in modern-day New England.

1603 Queen Elizabeth dies in the spring.

1604 England's King James I establishes treaty with Spain that recognizes the right of English merchants to deliver their ships to Spanish colonies for trade; that same year, Captain John Smith returns from his years as a mercenary soldier in eastern Europe.

1606 English merchants establish Virginia Company of Plymouth and the Virginia Company of London to colonize in North America; by year's end, the Virginia Company of London (the London Company) is ready to deliver colonists to America; their three ships set sail in December for the New World.

1607 *May* The London Company colonists establish their colony on the James River.

September Half of the 104 English colonists at Fort James have died.

Winter Captain John Smith has famous encounter with Chief Powhatan and his daughter Pocahontas.

1608 Popham Colony in New England fails.

January Only 38 of the original 144 men who sailed to establish colony at Jamestown the previous year are still alive; later that year, Captain John Smith pens his first important report of Jamestown, *A True Relation of Such Occurrences and Accidents of Noate as Hath Hapned in Virginia.*

1609 London Company officials convince King James I to abolish the local council government of Jamestown in favor of one-man rule—a governor; that fall, John Smith is seriously wounded in an accidental gunpowder explosion.

October Smith is taken back to England to recover, never to see Jamestown again.

1609–10 Through that winter, the Jamestown colonists experience "the Starving Time."

1610 In May, the population of Jamestown is 60, approximately 10 percent of the 600 people who had arrived in Jamestown as colonists over the previous three years; Sir Thomas Dale and Sir Thomas Gates are sent to Jamestown to get the colony on its feet.

June Even as the remnant colonists are preparing to abandon Jamestown, new colonists arrive under the leadership of Governor Lord Delaware.

1611 *March* Governor Delaware leaves Jamestown and is replaced by Sir Thomas Dale, who brings a new level of discipline to the colony; this same year, English colonial leader John Rolfe introduces Caribbean tobacco to Virginia creating the colony's first cash crop.

1613 In an English raid, Chief Powhatan's daughter Pocahontas is taken as a prisoner to Jamestown.

1614   Captain Smith returns to America, this time to explore New England; earlier that year, John Rolfe and Pocahontas are married.

1616   John Rolfe takes Pocahontas to England; during their tour, Pocahontas dies of smallpox.

1618   Jamestown and Virginia colonists produce almost 50,000 pounds of tobacco for export; that same year, Chief Powhatan dies.

1619   First large group of women are brought to the Jamestown colony; they marry colonists and produce the colony's first English children; that same year, Sir Edwin Sandys gains the leadership of the London Company; he will replace Governor Dale with Sir George Yeardley; Virginians also gain the right to elect some of their own leaders who will meet in the House of Burgesses; a Dutch ship delivers a "cargo" of 20 African workers to Jamestown.

1619–1625   Four thousand English colonists flock to make their homes in Virginia, including Jamestown.

1620   English colonists aboard the *Mayflower* land at Plymouth, New England.

1622   *March* Chief Opechancanough launches a series of attacks that result in the deaths of more than 300 colonists up and down the James River.

1624   John Smith publishes his *Generall Historie of Virginia*; that same year, King James I cancels the London Company's charter and turns Virginia into a royal colony; the House of Burgesses is dissolved.

1625   Approximately 1,300 colonists call Virginia their home; they are living in 21 different settlements along the James River and the Eastern Shore.

1625–1640   Approximately 1,000 indentured servants reach the Tidewater region each year.

1639   After being dissolved by James I in 1624, the House of Burgesses is reestablished.

1640 Tobacco exports from Virginia to England reach 1 million pounds.

1644 An aging Chief Opechancanough organizes another series of attacks, which bring about the deaths of 400 colonists.

1646 Chief Opechancanough dies.

1660s–1670s Virginia laws are written to define blacks as permanent slaves.

1670 Virginia, including Jamestown, is home to approximately 30,000 colonial residents, while Native Americans number only 6,000.

1676 Jamestown is burned by a party of discontented Virginians protesting the policies of the colony's governor.

1695 Construction begins on the College of William and Mary at Middle Plantation, several miles from Jamestown.

1698 The College of William and Mary opens; on October 31, a fire engulfs Jamestown.

1699 Jamestown is abandoned as the capital of Virginia; Williamsburg becomes the new capital.

Notes

Chapter 1

1. James Horn, *A Land As God Made It: Jamestown and the Birth of America* (New York: Basic Books, 2005), 48.
2. Ibid., 8.
3. Ibid., 13
4. Carl Bridenbaugh, *Jamestown, 1544–1699* (New York: Oxford University Press, 1980), 3.

Chapter 2

5. Ibid., 6.
6. Ibid.

Chapter 3

7. Peter Charles Hoffer, *The Brave New World: A History of Early America* (Boston: Houghton Mifflin Company, 2000), 119.
8. Ibid.
9. Ibid., 120.
10. Horn, 27.
11. Ibid.
12. Ibid.
13. Tim McNeese, *The American Colonies* (St. Louis: Milliken Publishing Company, 2002), 8.

Chapter 4

14. Quoted in Horn, 34.
15. Ibid., 35.
16. Ibid., 39.
17. Ibid.
18. Ibid., 40.

Chapter 5

19. Ibid., 43.
20. Ibid., 42.
21. Ibid., 44.
22. Ibid., 45.
23. Ibid.
24. Ibid.
25. Allan Weinstein and R. Jackson Wilson, *Freedom and Crisis: An American History* (New York: Random House, Inc., 1974), 61.
26. Ibid.
27. Ibid., 62.
28. Giles Milton, *Big Chief Elizabeth: The Adventures and Fate of the First English Colonists in America* (New York: Farrar, Straus and Giroux, 2000), 270.

Chapter 6

29. Harold B. Gill and Ann Finlayson, *Colonial Virginia* (Nashville, Tenn.: Thomas Nelson, Inc., 1973), 15.
30. Ibid., 13.
31. Ibid.
32. McNeese, *The American Colonies,* 10.
33. Gill, 17.
34. Ibid., 18.
35. Ibid., 17.
36. Ed Southern, ed., *The Jamestown Adventure: Accounts of the Virginia Colony, 1605–1614* (Winston-Salem, N.C.: John F. Blair, Publisher, 2004), 91.
37. Gill, 18.

38. Southern, 90.

39. Ibid.

Chapter 7

40. McNeese, *The American Colonies*, 10.

41. Gill, 20.

42. McNeese, *The American Colonies*, 11.

43. Gill, 21.

44. Ronald P. Dufour, *Colonial America* (Minneapolis/St. Paul: West Publishing Company, 1994), 93.

Chapter 8

45. Horn, 196.

46. Ibid., 197.

47. Gill, 25.

48. Tee Loftin Snell, *The Wild Shores: America's Beginnings* (Washington, D.C.: National Geographic Society, 1974), 94.

Chapter 9

49. Gill, 34.

50. Ibid., 36.

51. Ibid., 38.

52. Ibid., 39.

53. Ibid., 41.

54. Horn, 279.

55. Ibid., 280.

56. Ibid.

57. Ibid., 282.

58. Bridenbaugh, 150.

Bibliography

Appelbaum, Robert, and John Wood Sweet. *Envisioning an English Empire: Jamestown and the Making of the North Atlantic World.* Philadelphia: University of Pennsylvania Press, 2005.

Athearn, Robert G. *The New World.* New York: Choice Publishing, 1988.

Boorstin, Daniel, ed. *Visiting Our Past: America's Historylands.* Washington, D.C.: National Geographic Society, 1977.

Bridenbaugh, Carl. *Jamestown, 1544–1699.* New York: Oxford University Press, 1980.

Commager, Henry Steele. *The American Destiny: An Illustrated History of the United States.* London: Orbis Book Publishing, 1986.

Dufour, Ronald P. *Colonial America.* Minneapolis/St. Paul, Minn.: West Publishing, 1994.

Geiter, Mary K., and W. A. Speck. *Colonial America From Jamestown to Yorktown.* New York: Palgrave Macmillan, 2002.

Gill, Harold B., and Ann Finlayson. *Colonial Virginia.* Nashville, Tenn.: Thomas Nelson, Inc., 1973.

Hoffer, Peter Charles. *The Brave New World: A History of Early America.* Boston: Houghton Mifflin, 2000.

Horn, James. *A Land As God Made It: Jamestown and the Birth of America.* New York: Basic Books, 2005.

Lange, Karen E. "Unsettling Discoveries at Jamestown: Suffering and Surviving in 17th Century Virginia." *National Geographic*, June 2002, 74–81.

McNeese, Tim. *The American Colonies.* St. Louis: Milliken Publishing Company, 2002.

——. *American Timeline: Settlement, 1607–1755.* St. Louis: Milliken Publishing Company, 1986.

——. *The Reformation.* St. Louis: Milliken Publishing Company, 1999.

Milton, Giles. *Big Chief Elizabeth: The Adventures and Fate of the First English Colonists in America.* New York: Farrar, Straus and Giroux, 2000.

Smith, Bradford. *Captain John Smith: His Life & Legend.* Philadelphia: J.B. Lippincott, 1953.

Snell, Tee Loftin. *The Wild Shores: America's Beginnings*. Washington, D.C.: National Geographic Society, 1974.

Southern, Ed, ed. *The Jamestown Adventure: Accounts of the Virginia Colony, 1605–1614*. Winston-Salem, N.C.: John F. Blair, 2004.

Weinstein, Allen, and R. Jackson Wilson. *Freedom and Crisis: An American History*. New York: Random House, 1974.

Further Reading

Alderman, Clifford Lindsey. *The Story of the Thirteen Colonies*. New York: Random House, 1966.

Broyles, Janell. *Timeline of the Jamestown Colony*. New York: PowerKids Press, 2004.

Collier, Christopher, and James Lincoln Collier. *The Paradox of Jamestown*. New York: Marshall Cavendish, Benchmark Books, 1998.

Doak, Robin S. *John Smith and the Settlement of Jamestown*. Minneapolis, Minn.: Compass Point Books, 2003.

Fritz, Jean. *The Double Life of Pocahontas*. New York: Marshall Cavendish, Grey Castle Press, 1991.

Sakurai, Gail. *The Jamestown Colony (Cornerstones of Freedom)* Danbury, Conn.: Scholastic (Children's Press), 1997.

Syme, Ronald. *John Smith of Virginia*. New York: William Morrow & Company, 1954.

Worland, Gayle. *Let Freedom Ring!: The Jamestown Colony*. Mankato, Minn.: Capstone Press, 2004.

Web sites

Jamestown Archaeological Project
www.apva.org/jr.html

The Jamestown Online Adventure
http://www.historyglobe.com/jamestown

Visiting the Jamestown Settlement
http://www.historyisfun.org/jamestown/jamestown.cfm

National Park Service Jamestown Site
http://www.jamestown.org/

Virtual Jamestown Project
http://www.virtualjamestown.org/

Picture Credits

Index

About the Contributors

Series editor and author **TIM MCNEESE** is associate professor of history at York College in York, Nebraska, where he is in his fifteenth year of college instruction. Professor McNeese earned an Associate of Arts degree from York College, a Bachelor of Arts in history and political science from Harding University, and a Master of Arts in history from Southern Missouri University. A prolific author of books for elementary, middle, high school, and college readers, McNeese has published more than 80 books and educational materials over the past 20 years, on everything from Picasso to landmark Supreme Court decisions. His writing has earned him a citation in the library reference work *Contemporary Authors*. In 2006, McNeese appeared on the History Channel program *Risk Takers/History Makers: John Wesley Powell and the Grand Canyon*.